BOOK OF
AMERICAN ANTIQUES

BOOK OF

Ian Bennett

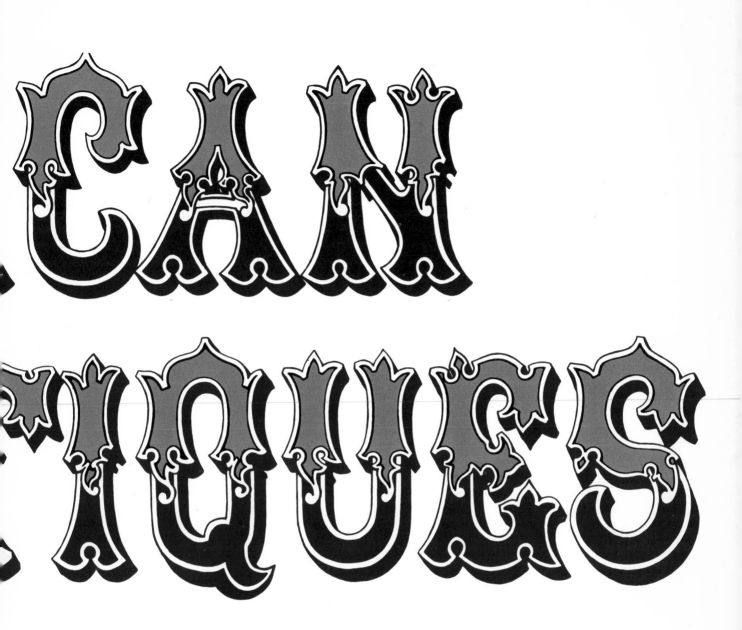

Hamlyn London New York Sydney Toronto

For Clare

Published by
The Hamlyn Publishing Group Limited
London · New York · Sydney · Toronto
Hamlyn House, Feltham, Middlesex, England

© Copyright The Hamlyn Publishing Group Limited 1973

ISBN 0 600 30130 3

Photo-typeset in England by
V. Siviter Smith & Company Limited
Printed in England by
Sir Joseph Causton & Sons Limited

Endpapers: 19th-century patchwork quilt

CONTENTS

1 Advertisement for the cabinetmakers and upholsterers Joseph Meeks & Sons, New York. The Metropolitan Museum of Art (Gift of Mrs R. W. Hyde, 1943).

2 Hartger's *View of New Amsterdam*, 1651. The New York Public Library.

For the collector, the span of American antiques may be safely described as a 150 year period between 1750 and 1900. The European concept of the antique as something which, almost mystically, must be over a hundred years old, has thankfully been losing ground for many years. Today we think of an antique work of art not necessarily as something which is very old, and therefore of necessity very valuable, but as an object which, through its intrinsic aesthetic merits, has withstood the onslaughts of fashion for long enough to give us reasonable hope that it is an example of something of enduring beauty.

Naturally, the closer something is to our own day, the less capable are we of judging it objectively. So rapidly have styles changed in the last seventy years, that Art Deco, made only forty or fifty years ago, seems as far from our own day as, say, the art of the Chippendale or Federal periods, although Art Deco has been dismissed as a mere 'fad' that will pass. It is certain, however, that a commentator in a hundred years time will feel a great deal safer in describing Art Deco as 'important' than anyone should feel today.

As we shall see in the following chapters, American art history dates back to the first settlers in New England in the first half of the 17th century, but for works of art to survive, they must be treated with respect – they must, in fact be thought of as objects in their own right, not merely as things with a use, to be discarded when they are outmoded or worn. It is just because the majority of 17th-century American artifacts were considered primarily as functional that so little has survived today. Except for examples of Pilgrim furniture, and wood of course is more durable than either glass or pottery, and not subject to the same economic pressures as silver, it is doubtful whether a new collector of Americana would find much on the market in the field of 17th-century works of art.

Apart from this, there is another reason why so few early American things have survived. Objects of luxury – fine silver, furniture, glass or ceramics, not to mention fine houses themselves – are the perquisites of wealth. Although America has always been a nominally classless society, a notion embodied in the famous saying that any American boy can become

President, wealth creates its own class, just as surely as any hierarchical structure based upon birth and inheritance. America has always been a country where fortunes could be made overnight and one characteristic of the *nouveau riche* is the desire for a degree of social acceptance in accord with their economic superiority.

Thus, to the rich merchant class of Colonial America, the ownership of English luxury goods was a manifest symbol of wealth and satisfied social aspirations. In the early Federal period, the pre-eminent sway of English influence was challenged by French styles, the new Republic of America having a fellow-feeling with the new Republic of France.

The American craftsman, with the exception of the furniture-maker, was largely spurned by the bourgeoisie of his own country until after the Revolution, and even then the way to success was an ability to follow the new styles of Europe as closely as possible. It is a remarkable fact that American craftsmen were able to create such individual styles in the face of such opposition. Even in the present century, the serious collecting of American works of art has been, until comparatively recently, confined to a few dedicated individuals. One has only to examine the auction records of a great saleroom like Parke-Bernet in New York, to see how little appreciated American art has been in the past.

In the last ten or twenty years, however, the growth of scholarly literature has brought home to Americans the richness of their own culture and we have seen an unprecedented boom in collecting and hence in prices. Nevertheless, whether you are a millionaire or a dedicated collector on a modest salary, the range is still wide. One can think of few areas of European art which offer such value for money as American bird decoys, 19th-century American glass, or American art pottery. The best Rookwood ceramics are considerably less expensive than English de Morganware or Pilkington Royal Lancastrian.

As yet, the supply of American late 18th- and 19th-century antiques is, in all but a few areas, ahead of the demand, but this is not a situation that can last forever.

FURNITURE

3 A Pilgrim oak chest, with carved tulip and sunflower motifs. Hartford, Connecticut, late 17th century.

Numbers in the margin refer to illustrations

The chief glory of American applied art is its furniture. From the earliest Pilgrim pieces of the 17th century to the splendid majestic designs of Frank Lloyd Wright some sixty-five years ago, American seat and case furniture has developed and encompassed a variety of styles and types. The peak was reached in Philadelphia towards the middle of the 18th century, when furniture of a richness and technical mastery not a wit inferior to the best efforts of English and French makers was produced. Throughout the 19th century, the brilliance of the late Federal styles gave way to eclectic mid-Victorianism, which in turn produced the finely designed pieces of the Arts and Crafts and Art Nouveau movements.

Most European countries which have produced fine furniture have had two traditions. On the one hand, there is the sophisticated town-made furniture produced by highly trained skilled craftsmen, the destination of which was the houses and palaces of the rich merchant classes and the aristocracy. But then there is what is usually described as 'provincial furniture', which appealed to the middle-class inhabitants of more rural areas. This was usually made by craftsmen of considerable technical ability who were, however, lacking in much originality. Nevertheless, this tradition could occasionally produce a maker of major significance, of whom the 18th-century French cabinetmaker Pierre Hache of Grenoble is probably the most famous.

In the United States, however, the situation, at least in the 18th century, the golden age of American furniture, was slightly different to that in Europe. The thirteen individual states of those days had an independence one from another which was based mainly on geographical considerations. While not actually pursuing a policy of isolationism towards each other, the inhabitants of each state did tend to live somewhat nationalistic lives, a policy which to a certain extent still pertains. The effect this had upon furniture was to make a 'provincial style', in the French or English sense, less obvious, certainly less separate from the sophisticated furniture of the cities.

Each of the major American furniture centres of the 18th century, Philadelphia, Boston, New York, Newport, and others, based their styles largely upon one common source—England. Thus while each centre developed its own idiosyncratic features, it had a common frame of reference which gave the effect of creating a number of centres, as opposed to England itself, where if you were not a London maker you were, by definition, provincial. For these reasons, provincial American furniture does not have a significant place in the history of the craft.

As if to compensate for this, America did produce one extremely important alternative tradition, namely Shaker furniture. Outside the United States, there is a surprising lack of knowledge about this sect and the really extraordinary dynamism of its furniture. In recent years, a number of studies of the functionalist aesthetic have drawn the attention of European readers to Shaker crafts but they still have not received the international respect to which their brilliance entitles them. They were truly amongst the pioneers of modern design, albeit unwittingly. But before discussing their work in detail, we must chart the mainstream of American furniture.

American furniture from the 17th to the end of the first quarter of the 19th century admits to five main periods, each one of which is stylistically separate yet leads logically into the next. They are, with approximate dates, the Pilgrim period 1660–1700, William and Mary 1700–25, Queen Anne 1725–55, Chippendale 1755–85 and Federal 1785–1820. After this latter date, the rise of industrial methods and the resurrection of numerous styles of the past produced a type of furniture which is recognisable through its eccentricity. It was most frequently brash and lacking in restraint, leading to an exaggerated concern with superfluous decoration; a few individual makers, however, did produce pieces of great beauty. In general the period between 1830 and 1870 is not the happiest one for the applied arts in any country, although the Arts and Crafts movement which grew up in the 1870s produced a new approach based upon traditional values which revived the art of the furniture-maker.

The earliest American furniture which survives dates from the second half of the 17th century and, not surprisingly, mostly originated in Massachusetts and Connecticut. Towns such as Plymouth and Ipswich in the former state and Hartford in the latter, produced solid pieces based upon late 16th- and early 17th-century European styles. The most popular wood was oak, as it was in Europe, although the American variety was lighter in colour than its European counterpart, while maple and pine were also used. Nevertheless the American craftsman was not content to merely imitate European pieces. Although he used their forms and decorative motifs, he used them in an imaginative way. Thus what resulted was not completely original but it was something distinctly American which could never be mistaken for English, Dutch or German.

These early pieces are mainly chests, cupboards, tables and chairs, indeed the basic essentials of furnishing a house. The chests are usually elaborately, if roughly, carved in a manner which harks back to their Gothic and Renaissance antecedents. Particularly popular were flower motifs such as the tulip and the more famous sunflower, the latter being used as a generic name for these types of pieces. The earliest recorded maker of the New World is one Nicholas Disbrowe who was born in Essex, England in about 1612 and who came to America in the 1630s, setting himself up as a 'cutter and joyner' in Hartford, Connecticut. By a happy historical accident, the one piece by him to have survived, the famous chest which he fashioned for Mary Alleyn, is signed. This is generally held to have been produced in about 1680 and is of great historical importance as the first known piece of signed American furniture.

The other great documentary piece is the carved and painted chest of drawers made in 1678, which is now in the Winterthur Museum and is the earliest dated example of American furni-

ture to have survived. Probably made by Thomas Dennis of Massachusetts, its first owners were John and Margaret Stamford, whose initials appear carved on the chest's front; they were probably given it as a wedding gift. This chest of drawers is in fact an extraordinarily elaborate piece of furniture, boldly painted and carved with the strapwork motifs current in Europe a century earlier.

John Carver, first governor of the Plymouth plantation, and William Brewster, an elder of the same, both gave their names to distinctive 17th-century American chairs. The Carver chair has turned, round stretchers and the back contains three horizontal turned rails backed by three uprights; it has a rush seat. The Brewster chair, a variation on the Carver, has only two centre uprights in the back. These chairs were made up until the turn of the century when the ubiquitous ladderback appeared.

In Boston, the first recorded cabinetmaker, John Clark, became active at the beginning of the 1680s, although the mercantile activity of the town before that date is shown by the edict promulgated by the ruling body in 1660 that 'no person shall henceforth open a shop in the town, nor occupy any manufacture or science, till he hath completed 21 years of age, nor except that he hath served seven years apprenticeship, by testimony under the hands of sufficient witnesses'. The apprentice system, of course, was vital to the maintenance of high standards in all areas of manufacturing and the system in America was well organised, although 18th-century newspapers are littered with aggrieved craftsmen offering rewards for runaway apprentices. Nevertheless, the system was undoubtedly responsible for the rapid growth of the arts in America and for the high standards which they achieved.

Two communities who produced their own distinctive furniture were the Dutch colonists of New Amsterdam, and the Germans who settled in Pennsylvania. Typically Dutch is the large heavy wardrobe standing on big bun-shaped feet known as a *kas*, while the Germans are noted for their chests which were painted in strong, vivid colours. Symbolism played a major part in the decoration, especially on dower chests–for instance hearts signified happiness, stars luck, doves peace and so on. This type of chest continued to be made up until the 19th century, which shows the strength of the folk tradition in America.

The William and Mary style, introduced into America at the turn of the century, followed the same lines as in England. Oak remained popular, although the use of new woods added richness; the earliest signed piece of furniture from Philadelphia, the fall front desk by Edward Evans now at Colonial Williamsburg, employs walnut, a particularly popular wood at this time, as were red pine and white cedar. Rich veneers were also introduced, although this technique was widely practiced only during the Federal period.

American craftsmen at this time began to show a high degree of sophistication and also broadened the range of their pieces. One of the most celebrated American furniture forms, the highboy, made its debut during the William and Mary

period, the earliest examples having six turned legs. The lowboy, essentially a highboy without its top half, also appeared, as well as the slope-top desk and the upholstered armchair, or easy chair. Early 18th-century spice chests have similar bases to the lowboy but have a single-panelled door in the top half as opposed to the highboy's rows of drawers. The elaborate knopped and balustered legs of these pieces, and their wavy stretchers, give them a restless, Baroque appearance.

The feel of Queen Anne furniture, the first great style in America, presents a contrast to the 'restless' quality of the William and Mary period. It is based around the English painter and engraver William Hogarth's 'line of beauty', the smooth, flowing cyma or s curve. The richness of American Queen Anne pieces, and their superb craftsmanship, lifts the standard of furniture being made in the New World onto an entirely new level; the early 18th century produced cabinetmakers who were capable of transforming English styles into a unique and wonderful thing of their own.

This is not only a question of the inevitable development of a single craft, the fruits of hard-earned experience. By the beginning of the 18th century, the ports of New England had become important centres of trade and supported a rich and growing class who hankered after the elegant living their English counterparts were enjoying. Discussing Boston society in 1718, Daniel Neal wrote: 'A Gentleman from London would almost think himself at home in Boston when he observes the number of people, their houses, their furniture . . . there is no fashion in London but in three or four months it is to be seen in Boston.' This last sentence reflects, of course, the marked preference amongst the wealthy classes for imported goods, especially luxury items for the home, a preference which continued unabated until the fervent chauvinism of the post-Revolutionary period when the native craftsman enjoyed the benefits of an expanding economy.

Nevertheless, the natural resources of timber available to the furniture-maker in America were virtually limitless; once he had matched these with skill, he produced furniture in no way inferior to English pieces. Among American craftsmen in all fields, the furniture-maker probably had the greatest domestic success.

That furniture of good quality was deeply respected is demonstrated by the amusing testament of 1768, quoted by Joseph Downs in his classic book on the furniture of the Queen Anne and Chippendale periods, in which Caleb Pell of Pelham Manor left '. . . to my dau. Ann Laurence a negro girl and a Mahogany Chest of Drawers and a dining table and a tea table to be made for her. To my wife a negro boy and woman and child . . . also my two best beds with furniture and a mahogany tea table and a dozen best chairs . . . my silver plate, Looking glass and China'. The careful itemisation of the furniture, intermingled with the slaves, clearly shows the priorities of a merchant's possessions. It also shows how, with the coming of a rich bourgeoisie and a concomitant high standard of living, the range of furniture necessary to a well-appointed house increased. With this growth of demand came

6 Windsor fan-back armchair, New England, 18th century.

7 A pair of Queen Anne walnut balloon-seat side chairs. Philadelphia, about 1720–40.

8 Chippendale mahogany kettle-base chest of drawers, a form unique to Boston. About 1760–80.

6   7

8

9 The Hazard family Chippendale
carved mahogany bonnet-top highboy
by John Goddard, Newport, Rhode
Island, about 1760–80.

10 The unique form of the
Goddard-Townsend claw-and-ball foot.

9   10

a new breed of highly skilled craftsmen to cater to the wealthy
domestic market.

During the 18th century, Philadelphia became supreme in
the realm of furniture-making. The list of its outstanding
makers include Thomas Affleck, Jonathan Gostelowe, who is
credited with being the inventor of the distinctive serpentine
and flute-cornered chest of drawers, Thomas Tufft, William
Savery, Adam Hains, Benjamin Randolph, one of the greatest
makers of seat furniture of any country or age, James Gilling-
ham and James Folwell. In addition, a host of minor makers
added to the intense creative richness of the period.

Other cities, however, produced outstanding craftsmen. The
twenty generations of the Townsend-Goddard families of
Newport, Rhode Island, one of the most remarkable pheno-
mena in the history of the applied arts, elevated the furniture
of that region to a level of equality with Philadelphia, while
John Gaines and Samuel Dunlap II may be said to have
achieved the same high standards in New Hampshire, and
Benjamin Frothingham and John Cogswell in Boston.

The great age of New York furniture was not to come until
the end of the century, reaching its apogee with the work of
Duncan Phyfe. Nevertheless, the list of surviving craftsmen
indicates an active and creative environment with the blend
of Dutch, French and English influences producing a style of
furniture which, like New York silver, is distinctly ornate.

Other areas which were to become active only after the
Revolution were Baltimore and Charleston, South Carolina,
although the latter did produce one famous pre-Revolutionary
cabinetmaker in Thomas Elfe. Nevertheless, no labelled
example of pre-Revolutionary Charleston furniture has survived. Virginia, isolated from the sophisticated mainstream of
city furniture, produced some rather rustic pieces. Some of
them are of extremely high quality.

The characteristics of Queen Anne furniture are similar to   7
those which distinguish the silver of the period – strong, simple
forms which through the very boldness of their shapes, give a
feeling of great strength and richness. At the beginning of the
period, oak and walnut, hitherto the most frequently used
woods, began to give way in popularity to mahogany, which
was first used in quantity in Charleston, South Carolina and
which remained by far the most popular wood until the Federal
period. It should be noted, however, that walnut still played
an important role in the Queen Anne period and was often
used on more elaborate pieces in Philadelphia right through
the Chippendale period, while in New York the handsome
wood of the wild black cherry was even more popular than
mahogany.

Perhaps the most well-known types of American furniture,
pieces which exemplify the controlled elegance of the
American interpretation of the Queen Anne and Chippendale
styles, are the highboy and its companion lowboy (Professor
Downs has pointed out that the words highboy and lowboy   13
were coined in the 19th century, no instance of their use
being known in 18th-century literature) and the various forms
of chairs. As we have already noted, the highboy and lowboy

made their debuts during the William and Mary period, but in the mid 18th century, the six leg support was superceded by four high cabriole legs. Other distinctive features are the high, scrolling, breakfront top with the central, intricately carved, crest, corner flaminaires and the central carved shell of the bottom half.

It is generally agreed that the greatest American piece of furniture is the sumptuous van Pelt highboy now in the Winterthur Museum, executed in Cuban mahogany in Philadelphia between 1765 and 1780. This piece caused a sensation at the Howard Reifsnyder sale in New York in April 1929 when it was sold for $44,000, a price which was to remain the auction record for American furniture for nearly forty years.

Highboys are mainly associated with Philadelphia, just as the famous 'kettle base' form for the chest of drawers appears to be unique to Boston. In New York, the highboy was rarely made, although the chest-on-chest, resting upon feet, was extremely popular. Highboys were also not made in either the Carolinas or Virginia.

American chairs are seen at their finest in the form called in the United States 'easy chair', which is an adaptation of the French *bergère*. A specifically American variety of chair is the high, square-backed armchair known as the 'Martha Washington', while the so-called 'slipper' or 'lady's' chair has a low seat, usually twelve to fourteen inches from the floor, so that diminutive females would have no trouble in sitting elegantly upon it. Triangular corner chairs, which were made throughout the 18th century, were sometimes called 'writing' chairs or 'barber's' chairs.

In America, unlike France or England, there appears to have been no clear-cut distinction between makers of seat furniture and case furniture, although most important European workshops produced both. Thus Robert Barton, a Philadelphia maker, can probably be taken as typical of the many sided activities of the 18th-century craftsmen. His advertisement in the *Philadelphia Gazette* of August 9, 1739, states that he 'made and sold . . . near the Post Office in Philadelphia, at the most reasonable rates, Walnut, Mahogany, Easy, close-stool and slip-chairs, and stools, couches, settees, Backgammon tables, with men, boxes and dies. Who has a likely negro woman fit for town or Country Business, with a child about one year and an half old, to dispose of. Also right good Neatsfoot Oyl for coach and chaise leather and Harnesses to sell reasonably by the gallon or larger quantity.' Mr Barton would appear to have been a maker of seat and case furniture, an amateur slave-trader, saddler and tanner all in one!

It should be noted that many cabinetmakers did own slaves, who were employed as handymen, especially in the Southern states. Thomas Elfe from Charleston is known to have hired out skilled slaves to other local makers.

One of the most characteristic features of English and American furniture, the claw-and-ball foot, was certainly employed by American makers during the Queen Anne period, although it did not find its way to Connecticut and Massa-

chusetts much before the 1770s. The Goddard-Townsend families of Newport were particularly fond of this motif and developed it into a unique form of their own; on their pieces, a 9,1 very realistically modelled claw rests upon the ball, rather than grasps it, with long talons carved away from the ball's surface. These families are also noted for their superbly carved shell motifs, almost hallmarks of their furniture.

Certain features differentiate the chairs of one region from another. Thus Pennsylvania examples usually have spoon backs with solid splats and horseshoe-shaped seats, while New York chairs have wide splats and sloped rear feet, with cabriole front legs ending in straight stumps. One characteristic of the Philadelphia armchair is the positioning of the front legs, which are not located at the angles of the seat but face forwards; the arms of these easy chairs sometimes scroll outwards, a most unusual feature.

In the late 1760s and 1770s, the Chinese and neo-Gothic motifs made popular by Chippendale in England, appeared in Philadelphia, where the supremely elegant carving of its prod- 17 ucts easily differentiates them from the more stolid, Dutch-influenced, pieces made in New York. Chairs from Maryland 14 and Virginia, like those from Pennsylvania, are generally fairly heavy and unsubtle. These so-called 'Chester County' pieces demonstrate the lack of sophisticated craftsmen in such places, although they are frequently of good quality and are attractive to modern collectors not only because they are uncommon but also because they tend to be less expensive than the products of Philadelphia, Boston and New York.

One of the rarest forms of early 18th-century American furniture is the bed. In general, beds made during the Queen Anne and Chippendale periods were four-posters with festooned hangings; it is likely that in later years, especially in the Empire period when low sleigh-beds were fashionable, these early pieces were sold or broken up by their owners, in the same way as much 18th-century silver was melted down. Also, as Professor Downs has pointed out, early houses were continually burning down which, added to what we have just said, probably explains why so few examples have survived.

In the 1760s the feather mattress was challenged by the hair variety, as evinced by John Mason's extraordinary advertisement of 1769, a piece of 'hard-sell' copy in the best traditions of the advertising media! 'For sale Mattrasses, or wool beds, which are so beneficial to mankind for when a constitution grows weak through inadvertency, or any waye thrown to Confusion, these beds are of great use to rest on, therefore I would advise every constitution to be provided with one of them . . . [it] gives a greater spring to the nerves than feather beds.' It is interesting to note that concealed beds folding into the wall or behind curtains are not 20th-century inventions but were popular during the 18th century, when they were called 'deception' beds, a name too easy to misinterpret in our own day!

Unlike the French cabinetmakers, American furniture-makers rarely branded their names onto their pieces, relying on glued paper labels. Although a large number of pieces thus 11

11 A Hepplewhite inlaid mahogany card table by Elisha Tucker, Boston, about 1790.

12 Elisha Tucker's original label from the card table.

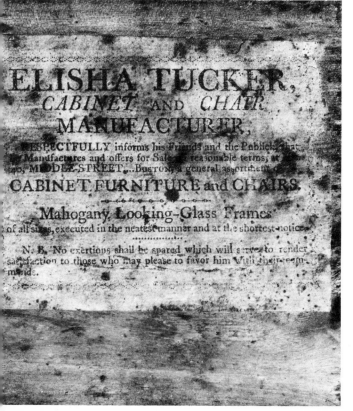

signed have survived, it was, from the modern historian's point of view, an unfortunate habit since the vast majority of such labels have become detached, which accounts for the relatively low number of things which can with absolute certainty be attributed to a given maker.

Also the label itself is no guarantee that the maker whose name appears upon it actually made the piece of furniture itself–it merely denotes the fact that it emanated from his workshop and thus bears his company's brand name. The discovery of a piece of signed furniture by the Scottish-born Philadelphia maker Thomas Affleck initially caused a mass of unsigned furniture in the same style to be attributed to him until it was realised that the signed piece was merely conforming to a standard Philadelphia taste, rather than vice versa.

During the Federal period, the American furniture-maker was able to follow more closely the styles current in London due to the increased amount of literature and pattern books available to them. Hepplewhite's *The Cabinet Maker's and Upholsterer's Guide* and Sheraton's *The Cabinet-Maker and Upholsterer's Drawing Book* of 1793–94, had enormous influence, as did *The London Cabinet-Makers' Book of Prices and Designs for Cabinet Work* of 1788. This was followed by *The London Chair-Makers' and Carvers' Book of Prices for Workmanship* of 1802, although a manuscript notebook of Philadelphian origin, *Prices of Cabinet and Chair Work* survives from 1786; not surprisingly, all the pieces described in it are of Queen Anne or Chippendale type. By 1792, the Americans had printed their own book of prices to be followed in 1794 by *The Philadelphia Cabinet and Chair-Makers' Book of Prices*. The dissemination of so much literature ensured the rapid growth of new styles in all the major towns and in so doing, increased the quality of workmanship and the size of the industry as a whole.

Throughout the 18th century, mahogany became increasingly used for fine furniture and Professor Charles Montgomery, in his book on Federal furniture in the Winterthur Museum, has estimated that between 1790 and 1825, seventy-five percent of the best furniture, with the exception of chairs, was made of this wood, provided that the furniture originated from cities with easy access to the sea or a major waterway, since mahogany could only be transported in bulk by ship.

Pittsburgh makers, for instance, continued to use walnut, as did craftsmen in more rural areas throughout the 18th century. Cherry remained popular in Connecticut and west Massachusetts while birch and maple tended to be reserved for less expensive pieces. A specifically American variety of maple called 'bird's eye' or 'curly', which has bold, strong markings, was occasionally used and such pieces are now highly appreciated by collectors. The wood itself was exported in great quantity to England, where it was used to make furniture and, extensively, picture frames. In England, this was the great age of satinwood furniture but American pieces of this wood are extremely rare.

American Federal furniture is also characterised by its use

13 The Beaver Chippendale carved walnut lowboy. Philadelphia, 18th century.

14 New York Chippendale carved mahogany five-leg gaming table, about 1760–85.

15 Federal inlaid mahogany gentleman's secretary and bookcase with *verre églomisé* decoration typical of Baltimore craftsmen. About 1790–1810.

16 One chair from the set of eight Sophia Miles Belden carved mahogany side chairs by Duncan Phyfe, New York, about 1810–20.

24 of vari-coloured veneers and inlays. Crotch mahogany, a highly figured variety of Cuban mahogany cut from the branches of the tree, was the most favoured wood for veneers and gave a rich lustrous glow when finished. Into this were often inlayed pictures or geometric patterns made of contrasting coloured woods, or inlayed lines of contrasting woods, a technique known as 'stringing'. The most ubiquitous forms of decorated inlay are the radiating oval, shell-like shapes called 'paterae', which, in contemporary American books, became synonymous with the whole process of inlaying under the name 'patries'.

The shape of American furniture at this time can, as we have said, be linked directly to the various books published in England in the 1780s and 1790s. The use of reeding in the supports is especially associated with Sheraton, whose influence produced more solid pieces than the light and lyrical aesthetic of Hepplewhite; the latter's furniture designs, emphasising the use of decorative inlays, tend towards the feminine and delicate and more immediately typify Federal furniture in the mind's eye. Amongst the greatest makers of furniture of the Sheraton type were John and Thomas Seymour of Boston.

One of the main influences in America at the turn of the century was the Greek revival pioneered in England by Adam, which for patriotic reasons – the popular association of Greece with liberty – became widespread after the adoption of the Federal Constitution in 1788. In France, the angular *Style Etrusque* of the late Louis XVI period, which laid emphasis upon straight lines and restrained decoration, had a strong influence upon English and later American craftsmen. Amongst the leading American makers in this style was Antoine-Gabrielle Quervelle of Philadelphia.

Not surprisingly, the earliest manifestations of the Federal style appeared in Philadelphia in the 1770s and 1780s, although by the end of the period, the focus of furniture-making had shifted from Philadelphia to New York which, throughout the 19th century, was to remain the most important American city, socially, politically and artistically.

Professor Montgomery considers the small desk made in Philadelphia by Benjamin Randolph for Thomas Jefferson in 1776 (now in the Smithsonian Institution, Washington) to be the earliest, clearly definable example of the Federal style, because of its angular delicacy and use of inlays, but it is clear that this was an isolated example at this date since the next piece to conform clearly to the new style is the piano case by Charles Albrecht of Philadelphia, which was not made until 1789. After this date, the Federal style gained rapid currency and the following year, Charles Shipley, a New York maker, advertised a full-blown vase-backed chair with the central 'Prince of Wales' motif of three feathers, which was to become a favourite decorative element on American Federal chairs. The three feathers surrounded by elaborately carved falling drapery is most usual in pieces made by the greatest cabinet-maker of the age, Duncan Phyfe of New York who also pioneered the wide-spread use of the lyre-back chair.

18

The increased use of intricate decorative elements gave rise to at least one great carver, Samuel McIntyre of Salem, whose work, consisting of superbly executed floral motifs, baskets of fruit, putti, indeed all the panoply of the late Baroque, is easily recognisable. His greatest achievement is the decoration on the chest-on-chest made by William Lemon for the Salem merchant Elias Hasket, now in the Karolik Collection at the Museum of Fine Arts, Boston, a piece considered to be amongst the masterpieces of the American cabinetmaker's art.

One of the most characteristic types of early 19th-century furniture are the painted pieces in the Grecian style mainly associated with Baltimore craftsmen such as John and Hugh Findlay, who also inset their pieces with *verre églomisé* (reverse-painted glass) panels. Some idea of how these colourful pieces look may be gained from the advertisement contained in the *Federal Gazette and Commercial Daily Advertiser* of November 8, 1805, in which the possible decorations are listed as 'real views, Fancy landscapes, Flowers, Trophies of Music, War, Husbandry, Love etc... Window and recess seats, painted and gilt in the most fanciful manner, with or without views adjacent to this city'.

From 1810 onwards, the angular delicacy of English-influenced furniture gave way to the Empire style, first popularised in France and notable for its great richness which, in the hands of some European makers, comes very close to being ostentatiously vulgar. The various influences which produced the Empire style include, above all, a transmutation of Neo-classicism, made more extravagant and solid, plus the new aesthetic resulting from the Napoleonic campaigns in Egypt of 1798. Sphinxes, caryatids, Greek key patterns, and abundant use of gilding upon rich, dark woods produced a furniture of unparalleled magnificence.

In New York, Duncan Phyfe adopted many of the motifs associated with the Empire style but his perfect sense of balance and restraint avoided the excesses committed by some European makers and his furniture is not fully Empire in the French sense of the word. Also in New York, however, Charles-Honoré Lannuier, a French cabinetmaker produced superb, fully developed Empire furniture as did Michael Allison and Joseph Meeks of the same city. The most ornate American Empire pieces were made by Joseph B. Barry in Philadelphia.

By the end of the first decade of the 19th century, the making of American furniture was ceasing to be a craft and was becoming an industry. Even by 1810, production had reached almost industrial proportions; the *Niles Weekly Register* of 1814 reported that in 1810, there were 482 cabinetmakers active in Pennsylvania who produced a total of just over $650,000 worth of chairs, about $12,000,000 in present money terms, while in Massachusetts in the same year, 8,368 chairs were made valued at $96,060. Even Maryland could support fifty cabinetmakers and produce $273,043 worth of furniture. By the middle of the 1830s, a unified furniture style was giving way to the wild eclecticism which typifies mid Victorian taste.

In America the wide variety of historical designs imported from Europe was compounded by the large number of Continental furniture-makers who emigrated during the mid century, especially from Germany and France. The 18th-century French revival was popularised by the Paris firm of Riguet Le Prince, who established showrooms in New York, while in the 1850s, the extravagant neo-Rococo of Louis-Philippe found favour in America, and was called either 'French Modern' or 'French Antique', a contradiction which typifies the jumbled mass of ideas being propounded at the time. Side by side with these styles were the Greek Revival, a sort of neo-Neo-classicism, neo-Gothic, neo-Tudor and Islamic. In New Orleans, that sophisticated French enclave outside the mainstream of North American cultural life, two makers, François Seignouret and Prudent Mallard produced extraordinarily rich Baroque furniture, unlike anything made elsewhere in the United States.

Two important figures in the history of American furniture are Lambert Hitchcock and John Henry Belter. Hitchcock, whose first enterprise was a factory making chair parts, established at Barkhamsted, Connecticut in 1818, is generally accredited with being the first manufacturer of mass-produced furniture. In 1825, Hitchcock moved his factory to a place he modestly named Hitchcockville, now Riverton, and began to produce his own furniture, rather than supply vast quantities of parts to other manufacturers. These inexpensive pieces have frames of maple or birch and were painted to simulate rosewood (his early examples) or ebony and were often stencilled in gold to suggest brass inlays.

The enterprise collapsed in 1828 but re-started soon afterwards, pieces made after this date being stamped 'Hitchcock, Alford & Co., Hitchcockville, Conn., Warranted', the Alford being Arba Alford who was taken into partnership in the newly formed company. This second attempt proved successful and in 1843, Hitchcock started an independent factory, which produced identical furniture, at Unionville, which lasted until his death in 1852; pieces made here are marked 'Lambert Hitchcock, Unionville, Conn.' Meanwhile, back at Hitchcockville, Arba had taken his brother Alfred Alford into partnership, and their pieces are marked 'Alford & Co.'; these continued to be made until 1846.

John Henry Belter, who was born in Württemberg, Germany, in 1804, emigrated to America in about 1840, along with many of his compatriots, and soon after, patented a method of producing laminated bentwood furniture by steam-compression methods. This system had been perfected in Europe by the German Michel Thonet, who had been producing bentwood chairs in the 1830s, and whose work was probably well-known to his compatriot. Belter started a company to make his furniture, which perhaps epitomizes high Victorian taste. He is known principally for his laminated rosewood parlour and bedroom suites, highly ornate with quantities of elaborate but perfectly executed carving.

In the 1870s, a number of designers and makers began preaching the gospel of the Arts and Crafts movement, inspired by two of the most influential aesthetic books of the 19th cen-

17 18th-century Chippendale mahogany highboy, showing the typical Philadelphian combination of detailed carving and rich dark wood.

18 A Pennsylvania Dutch marriage chest with painted decoration, 1780–90. The Henry Francis du Pont Winterthur Museum.

19 A rare Philadelphia Chippendale mahogany pie-crust tea table of about 1770.

20 New York Chippendale mahogany fire screen, about 1760, with its original needlework.

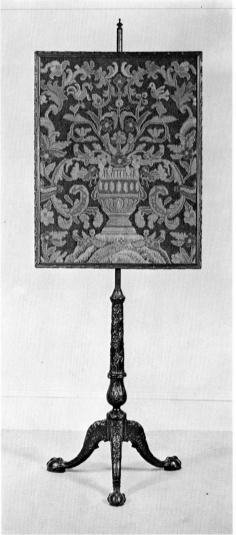

21 An accordian-fold dining table by Duncan Phyfe, New York, about 1810–20.

22 Federal cherrywood hunt board (small sideboard), about 1810–25. The plainness of this piece suggests a provincial origin, probably Virginia.

23 Side chair of hickory and ash, painted black with gilt stencilled decoration. By Lambert Hitchcock, about 1830. Private collection.

21

22   23

22

tury, Charles Lock Eastlake's *Hints on Household Taste*, published in England in 1868, and Edward W. Godwin's catalogue of 1877, which first propagated the Japanese ideals of design which were to have such widespread effect upon the applied arts of the late 19th century.

In New York, the firm of Christian Herter produced fine art furniture as did Isaac E. Scott of Chicago. In 1888, the firm of Tovey & Christiansen, an offshoot of the Tobey Furniture Company founded by the Englishman Charles Tobey, marketed extremely high-quality hand-made pieces, which showed, in their beautifully balanced construction, the influence of the Norwegian designer William F. Christiansen, who employed many of his own countrymen.

In the 1890s, the Arts and Crafts movement merged into the flowing, liquid style of Art Nouveau, and several American craftsmen, notably Gustav Stickley and Elbert Hubbard, the latter in his Roycroft Workshops at East Aurora, produced extraordinarily fine examples of this type. This was also a time when the concept of a house as a total unit–a concept not unfamiliar to Federal makers–began to have added meaning for architects, who were keen to design furniture to suit the carefully planned spaces of their rooms.

The greatest architect at the turn of the century was Louis Sullivan of Chicago, whose most distinguished pupil, Frank Lloyd Wright, established his own practice in 1893 and thereafter frequently designed superb, functionalist furniture for his clients' houses; one of his most famous pieces of furniture is the library table designed in 1908 for Ray W. Evans, which is now in the Art Institute of Chicago. Another of Sullivan's pupils, George Grant Elmslie, a Prairie School architect, also designed fine furniture, as did George Maher.

It is fitting that our discussion of the mainstream of furniture made in the United States should close on such a creative period in the history of American art.

The alternative tradition: Shaker furniture

The Shakers were a religious sect formed by Ann Lee, who, fleeing persecution in England, emigrated to America in 1774. For the next 150 years, they enriched the cultural life of their adopted country with their dedicated, inventive skill and produced, amongst other things, a style of furniture which has had tremendous influence upon the 20th-century approach to design.

Dedicated to a life of work and prayer, the Shaker communities believed that in order for a piece of furniture to serve the end for which it was intended, it should consist only of the necessary functional elements, any added decoration being mere pretentious frivolity.

This belief is embodied in a number of their writings where we find such phrases as: 'Anything may, with strict propriety, be called perfect which perfectly answers the purpose for which it was designed.' *The Laws of the Millennium*, which set down the rules of life to be obeyed by all who wished to be Shakers, states: 'Whatever is fashioned, let it be plain and simple, unembellished by superfluities which add nothing to its goodness and durability.' These two statements, taken together, form an extraordinary testament to the modernity of the Shakers' views. A hundred years before the Bauhaus they had succinctly formulated a doctrine of functionalism and, more importantly, put that doctrine into practice in a way which makes the apparently revolutionary theories of our day seem mere repetition. The Shakers were truly prophets in more ways than one.

Because the emphasis was placed upon functionalism and because, at the beginning of Shaker history in America at least, furniture was made to be used solely by the communities themselves, no concessions were made to fashionable styles, or indeed to any consideration other than usefulness. Thus once a satisfactory shape had been devised which was strong, functional, and essentially simple to make, it was passed on to the other Shaker settlements and continued to be made unchanged over the years. Thus, as John G. Shea remarks in his book on Shaker furniture: 'Some of the classic Shaker chairs and rockers first made during the early years of the 19th century, remained only slightly modified in their final production almost a century later.'

The 'classic Shaker chairs and rockers' mentioned here are indeed the most famous types of Shaker furniture and were produced in commercial numbers by the Shaker factory founded by Elder Robert Wagan in New York, which existed until the 1930s. The usual types are slat-backs with woven seats. Early pieces were woven with hickory splints and later ones with cane, rushes and brightly coloured strips of material, this latter being one of the Shakers' only concessions to 'Wordly Show'.

The earliest Shaker community at New Lebanon is known to have been producing furniture by 1789 and these first pieces included the great Shaker rocking-chairs, a type of seat furniture perfected by them. These were made with or without arms and came in a variety of sizes, ranging from very small examples for children to the 'Great Rockers' for adults. Early examples are now amongst the most highly regarded types of American furniture not only because of the superb workmanship they display, but also because they *do* serve perfectly the purpose for which they were intended.

Amongst other common types of American furniture, the chest of drawers often have a slight degree of ornamentation and are also very interesting because, unlike other forms, they are often signed. Thus some names of Shaker craftsmen have survived–Isaac Youngs of New Lebanon, Richard McNemar, leader of the Western Shakers, Micajah Burnett of Pleasant Hill, Kentucky, Brother Giles Avery, Elder Hervey L. Eads of South Union, Kentucky, Daniel Sering of Union Village, Ohio and Elder Joseph Myrick of Harvard.

These latter two makers are particularly important to students of Shaker furniture since the former signed a dresser in 1827 and the latter a chest in 1844, which are amongst the earliest documented pieces. The last Shaker craftsman,

24 A combined desk and bookcase, Connecticut or Rhode Island, about 1790–1810 and a Martha Washington chair, north-eastern Massachusetts or Portsmouth, about 1800. The desk and bookcase is of cherrywood with inlaid mahogany and light woods. The silk satin upholstery of the chair is 18th-century French. The Henry Francis du Pont Winterthur Museum, Winterthur, Delaware.

25 An outstanding example of Shaker furniture, this cherrywood pedestal table was made at the first settlement at New Lebanon, New York, in about 1820. The American Museum in Britain, Bath.

26 Library table designed by Frank Lloyd Wright in 1908 for the Ray W. Evans house in Chicago, Illinois. Art Institute of Chicago (Gift of Mr and Mrs F. M. Fahrenwald).

27 Laminated rosewood parlour suite by
John Henry Belter, New York, about 1850–60.

Brother Delmar C. Wilson of the Sabbathday Lake Community, Maine, who died in 1955, was well known for his carriers and boxes, forms which remained consistent throughout the 19th and 20th centuries.

But perhaps the most beautiful type of Shaker furniture is the pedestal table resting on a single baluster stem and three baluster legs (although a few examples have cross-lapped, four-legged bases). These brilliantly polished pieces, usually of maple or cherry if made in the East and walnut or cherry if made in the West, are perfect examples of how utter simplicity, combined with perfect craftsmanship, can produce works of art comparable in sophistication with anything made by the highly trained craftsmen working for a fashionable market.

One of the finest of these tables is in the American Museum **25** at Bath in England where it does not look out of place surrounded by the finest achievements of 18th-century Philadelphia, Boston and New York. This piece, like all Shaker furniture, is an enduring testament to a sincere and gentle people of whose sect there are now, sadly, only two survivors.

Clocks

The first important American clocks date from the mid 18th century, the two leading centres being Philadelphia and Boston, the former city producing the finer pieces. The majority of these were long-case clocks, called tall-case or **28** coffin clocks in America (the popular generic name grandfather clock did not become current until after Henry Clay wrote his famous song in 1876). Long-case pieces were first produced in Europe in the second half of the 17th century, and the earliest American examples usually contain English movements. The cases were also similar, the hoods being embellished with swan-neck pediments. In Connecticut, crested hoods, called 'whales' tails, were extensively used, and are most commonly associated with Thomas Harland, who moved to Norwich, Connecticut from Boston. His pupils included Daniel Burnap, a distinguished maker who worked at East Windsor, Connecticut.

Massachusetts case-makers were fond of open-fretwork decoration on the hood and three brass urn-shaped finials. This type is known as a Roxbury case. Miniature or 'dwarf' long-case clocks were also made at the beginning of the 19th century and are now extremely popular with collectors. Two makers from Hingham, Massachusetts, Reuben Tower and his brother-in-law Joshua Wilder, are especially associated with this type of case. It is worth noting that the bracket clock, perhaps the most brilliant example of English horological skill, was rarely made in America.

Among the earliest known American makers are Isaac Pearson of Burlington who was the proprietor of the Mount Holly Ironworks from 1730 to 1749, William Claggett and his son-in-law James Wady, both of Newport, Rhode Island and Edward Duffield of Philadelphia. The greatest figure, however, is David Rittenhouse of Norristown, Pennsylvania, who with his many interests in horology, astronomy, surveying,

28 Chippendale maple and curly maple long-case clock by Isaac Doolittle of New Haven, Connecticut, about 1760–80.

politics, etc., was a man of almost Renaissance stature. His two most famous pieces are the orreries he made for Princeton University and the University of Pennsylvania, the first of which dates from 1770.

Among the many celebrated cabinetmakers who produced cases for imported clocks are Edward James and John Folwell of Philadelphia, the latter making a case for one of the Rittenhouse orreries. John Townsend, a member of the Townsend-Goddard family of Newport, Rhode Island, made superb cases, as did Thomas Johnson, a japanner from Boston.

At the beginning of the 19th century, a severe shortage of metal necessitated the use of wooden mechanisms. Between 1807 and 1810, Eli Terry of Connecticut pioneered mass-production methods at his clock factory in New York, turning out roughly four thousand wood movements. A few years earlier, in about 1795, Simon Willard had designed his 'patent timepiece', a wall clock with a banjo-shaped case. Over the **30** next few years, he is known to have produced several thousand such pieces himself as well as farming out the right to produce such clocks to his favourite pupils, one of the best of whom was Elnathan Taber of Roxbury, Massachusetts; such pupil-made examples bear the words 'Willard's Patent'.

Willard's brother Aaron, of Grafton, Massachusetts, active between 1770 and 1823, produced square, bracket-type wall clocks, with scrolled feet resting upon a single wall bracket. The Massachusetts shelf clock and the Connecticut pillar- **29** and-scroll shelf clock, were also extremely popular timepieces during this period. In the 1830s, a variety of shelf clock with a single door, bronzed-looking glass and a painted glass panel in the lower part of the door, was developed by Chauncey Jerome.

Of the variations on Willard's original banjo clock, the most famous is the girandole version made by Lemuel Curtis, while 'diamond' banjo clocks, with angular heads, were produced in small numbers by such makers as Jabez Baldwin of Salem. Both this type and the girandole are rare today and much in demand amongst collectors. Another type of clock associated with Willard is the Eddystone Lighthouse alarm timepiece, which he designed in 1822, the body being in the shape of the famous edifice after which it is named. Only about fifty examples are known to exist today. In the 1840s, Edward Howard of Boston, a pupil in fact of Aaron Willard, produced his own version of the banjo, with the lower part of the clock being round instead of rectangular. He also made rectangular cased pieces with convex rather than flat sides which were extensively used on railway stations.

In the 1830s, the lack of metal was no longer a problem, and factory-made rolled brass began to be widely employed (although cast brass had always been used for the complicated mechanisms of eight-day pieces); the depression in 1837 finally forced most wooden clockmakers out of business. One of the major makers was Chauncey Jerome who, from 1838 onwards, produced inexpensive thirty-hour brass clocks in very large quantities, as did the other manufacturer who followed Jerome's lead, Seth Thomas. Many of Jerome's movements

29 Mahogany pillar-and-scroll clock with outside escapement and pictorial *verre églomisé* panel. By Eli Terry of Plymouth, Connecticut, about 1825.

30 Banjo clock of about 1840 by A. Willard Jnr. The American Museum in Britain, Bath.

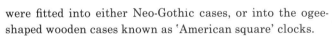

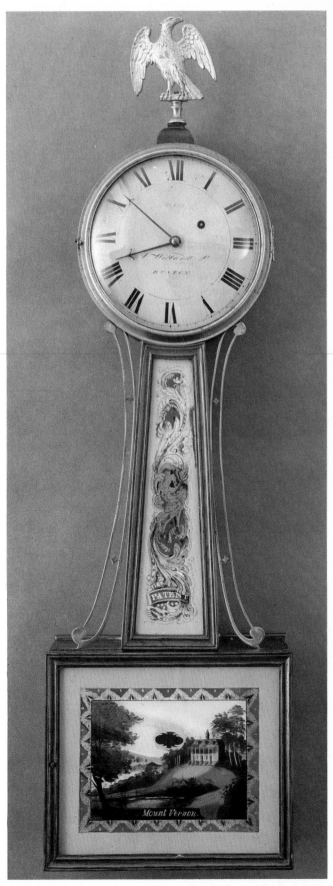

were fitted into either Neo-Gothic cases, or into the ogee-shaped wooden cases known as 'American square' clocks.

In the period between 1825 and 1850, a large number of spring clocks were made, utilising a mechanism devised by Joseph Ives on the principal of the leaf-spring used in carts and wagons. The best examples of this type were made by Birge and Fuller. Another popular type of clock was the acorn, so-called because of the shape of its gaily decorated case.

Later in the century, the craft of fine clockmaking in America gave way to novelty pieces of no great horological interest. Such firms as the Ansonia Watch Company of Ansonia, New York, produced exceptionally ornate, and somewhat vulgar, ormolu-cased pieces based upon French 18th-century models, while cast iron clocks in the form of animals, negro minstrels etc., were also made in large numbers. One or two fine Art Nouveau clocks were made but are of great rarity today.

ESSE QUAM VIDERI

31 Engraved silver beaker by John Hull and Robert Sanderson, Boston, about 1670.

32 Coffee pot by Myer Myers of New York, about 1760.

Fine silver has always been one of the most obvious signs of wealth and social prestige. In the young America it was only natural that silver should be anxiously accumulated by the rich merchant class as it had been in all the great centres of Europe from time immemorial.

There was, however, a far more practical connection between silver and wealth than there is today. When in 1969, there was a tremendous boom in collecting antique silver, several writers on the subject pointed out that because the price of 17th- and 18th-century silver was so much above the value of silver bullion, the connection between the latter and antique silver was more psychological than real. In the 17th century, nothing could have been more untrue. Silver was the metal of coinage but whereas the value of currency was often arbitrary and subject to sudden fluctuations, the value of silver itself remained reasonably constant; for this reason, a collection of silver was not only prestigious in itself but also served the practical purpose of an easily convertible asset.

The first settlers in the New World had made a permanent move. Therefore, they brought all their worldly goods with them and it is certain that, in addition to silver and gold coinage, they also brought quantities of silver plate. As they built up a way of life based upon that which they had known in Europe, the more successful amongst them required silversmiths not only to furnish them with plate, cutlery and drinking vessels but also to repair, or to render into coinage, pieces they had brought with them. Thus the silversmith, like the furniture-maker, was an essential servant of the new society.

The amount of surviving 17th-century American silver is, of course, comparatively small. Silversmiths are recorded as working in the years immediately following the landing of the Pilgrims, and John Mansfield of Charlestown, Massachusetts, is known from documents to have been active in 1634; but all the known pieces almost certainly date from the second half of the century.

The first clearly delineated figures in the history of American silver are John Hull and Robert Sanderson of Boston. Not **31,40** only did they make the most important surviving silver of this period but the greatest late 17th- and early 18th-century Boston makers were taught by them; indeed, it is a fortuitous circumstance that the presence of these makers in Boston assured the pre-eminence of that city in this particular field, as opposed to Philadelphia, the leading city for furniture and for the whole artistic 'life-style' of the 18th century.

John Hull was born in England in 1624, was brought to America at an early age and served his apprenticeship in Boston under his half-brother, Richard Storer, who had been trained in London but who had never completed his apprenticeship. The only piece which bears John Hull's mark alone is a tapered cylindrical beaker, a piece which might lay serious claim to being the only pre-1650 piece of American silver surviving.

Hull utilised his position as the leading silversmith in Boston (between about 1650 and 1680, the surprisingly high number of twenty-four makers are recorded as working in the city) to become a successful merchant and a leading member of the community. In 1652, he was appointed to the very important position of Master of the Massachusetts Mint and it was at this time that he took as his partner the other great protagonist in the history of American silver, Robert Sanderson.

Sanderson was born in London in 1608 and unlike Hull, had been trained there and had been an active maker before emigrating to America. In about 1659, Hull and Sanderson jointly made one of the most historically important pieces of American silver, a small beaker. This is dated 1659 and bears the pricked initials 'T/BC' standing for the Boston Church or the First Church, founded in 1630, in whose collection it remains to this day. The punched and matted decoration of this piece is typical of early Jacobean English silver and demonstrates the time lag between American and English designs.

Hull, after reaching social and economic eminence, died in 1682 and after this date, Sanderson carried on alone, as evidenced by a small number of pieces which bear his single mark. Less than forty pieces bearing Hull and Sanderson's joint mark survive today.

The following generation of Boston silversmiths included Jeremiah Dummer (1645–1718), John Coney (1655–1722), John Edwards (1671–1746) and Edward Winslow (1669–1753), of whom the first listed was Hull and Sanderson's first recorded pupil. But before discussing these makers' work, we should look at the situation in New York.

Although, as we said before, silver was an essential perquisite of riches, it should be remembered that many of the early American settlers had left their native countries because of religious differences and the lack of opportunity for free worship. Thus churches were important and central edifices within the new communities and, as in Europe, the practice of bequeathing silver to their local church was continued by the members of America's new mercantile class. For the modern student, this is a particularly happy circumstance; whereas domestic silver tended to have a short life, being frequently melted down for coinage or for remaking into more fashionable styles, churches have always carefully accumulated their gifts. Thus the majority of surviving 17th-century American pieces, not only from Boston, but also from New York, were made for nonconformist or Dutch Reformed Churches and in many cases are still retained by the individual churches for which they were made and to which they were bequeathed.

An added advantage for the student is that such gifts are usually inscribed with the name of the donor and the date the bequest was made. Such inscriptions are valuable guides to dating individual pieces, although, as every writer has pointed out, too much confidence in such dating is dangerous. It can often be demonstrated on stylistic grounds that a given piece was made sometime before it was given to the church, the date upon it merely recording the time it was given rather than the year it was made. With very few exceptions, American silver is impossible to date with the same accuracy as English silver,

since the compulsory hall-marking system of England was not adopted in America.

The settlers of New York, or New Amsterdam as it was called until 1664, were primarily of Dutch origin and thus the silver made there was of Dutch inspiration, as opposed to Boston silver, which was predominantly English in style. In addition to the Dutch, however, French settlers also brought a distinctive flavour to New York metalwork. The amount of New York silver of the 17th and early 18th centuries is considerably smaller than that surviving from Boston, a fact shown by the low number of such pieces held by churches – a mere eighteen.

The outstanding New York silversmiths of the 17th century were Cornelius van der Burch (about 1653–99), Jacobus van der Spiegel (emigrated 1668–died 1708), Ahasuerus Hendricks (active about 1675–80), his stepson Gerrit Onckelbag or Onclebagh (about 1670–1732), Jacob Boelen (about 1654–1729), Jurian Blanck Jnr (about 1645–1714), and one of the earliest and greatest emigrant Huguenot silversmiths, Bartholomew Le Roux (1663–1713).

There is an immediate stylistic difference between New York and Boston silver, a difference which remains, albeit to a lesser extent, throughout the 18th century. Dutch silver is far more ornate and highly decorated than English silver of the same period. The Dutch auricular style of Adam van Vianen (Utrecht 1565–1627) and his brother Paul, was one of the greatest contributions to European silverware and heralded the Baroque style at a time when English silver was still involved with the strapwork decoration of the Elizabethan period.

Thus in America it is interesting to compare the elegant but completely plain beakers of the Boston school to the similarly shaped but elaborately decorated New York pieces. Perhaps the most famous example of this latter type is the engraved beaker by Cornelius van der Burch, about 1685, now in the Yale University Art Gallery (the Mabel Brady Garvan Collection). This piece is totally Dutch in conception, with engraving based upon illustrations by the Dutch artist Adrien van der Venne (1589–1662) for the collected works of Jacob Cats, published in Amsterdam in 1655. The presence of scenes from so recently published prints upon a piece of American silver, which follows the Dutch silversmiths' practice of adapting paintings and engravings, as well as that of decorating tankards with lions' masks and ornately applied and chased bases, shows that the New York emigrants were fairly *au fait* with what was going on in Europe. The time lag of twenty to thirty years between styles appearing in Europe and their adoption in America remained constant until the Revolution, but slowly shortened thereafter.

In Boston, the greatest silversmith in the period between roughly 1680 and 1720 was unquestionably John Coney. As Graham Hood, in his book on American silver, says: 'His career spanned three different style periods and monumental examples by him in each style have fortunately survived. Virtually all the silver known to have been made by him is of

33 Tankard by Edward Winslow of Boston, engraved with the arms of the Hutchinson family of Massachusetts, about 1730.

33 Tankard by Edward Winslow of Boston, engraved with the arms of the Hutchinson family of Massachusetts, about 1730.

34 Tankard by Cornelius Kierstede, New York, about 1700.

fine quality, and his best objects are masterpieces of the art.'

His greatest pieces include small two-handled cups with caryatid handles adapted from English porringers of the late Carolingian period, some massive tankards, spout cups, some splendid two-handled cups and covers, including the exceptional example now in Harvard University (about 1701) in the William and Mary style, the magnificent William and Mary monteith bowl (about 1700–10), which is considered one of the greatest pieces of American silver, and a wide range of objects in the bold, strong, undecorated style of Queen Anne.

Coney's claim to greatness lies not only in his ability to produce pieces of a consistently high quality but also because of his proven ability to understand and adapt the widely differing styles of the William and Mary and Queen Anne periods. Looking at his famous sugar box of about 1700–15 in the Museum of Fine Arts, Boston, with its ornately chased and matted foliate decoration, its hinge lock adapted from cut-card work and its feet, which are in fact scrolled tankard thumbpieces, it is difficult to believe that the same maker a few years later could have made the beautifully functional and undecorated pear-shaped teapot in the Metropolitan Museum, New York.

The greatest number of surviving early American pieces are tankards. In Boston, as we would expect, tankards from the **33,34** 1680s and 1690s are monumental, plain and rely for effect upon balanced lines rather than on decoration. In New York, pieces by Cornelius Kierstede, Jacobus van der Spiegel and Jurian Blanck Jnr tend to have ornately engraved armorial cartouches, lids heavily ornamented with foliate engraving and reeded, foliate, bases. Even the earliest New York pieces, such as the example by Blanck in the Museum of the City of New York, are sufficiently decorated to allow of no confusion with Boston pieces. Another New York characteristic, most frequently seen in the work of Jacob Boelen, is the insetting of coins into the lids of tankards.

If tankards are among the most frequently found types of early American silver, some of the rarest pieces are candlesticks. Only one pair survives from the last decades of the 17th century. This, by Jeremiah Dummer, is now at Yale, and is in the beautifully elegant Corinthian column style associated with Charles II. It is interesting to note that even by 1715, the latest date that can be put upon the typically ornate pair of New York sticks by Cornelius Kierstede in the Metropolitan, the Corinthian style was still current in America, although turned baluster sticks were being fashioned at the same time by John Coney of Boston.

It is not surprising that the William and Mary style did not have such marked effect in New York as it did in Boston. New York silversmiths were, as we have pointed out, predominantly of Dutch origin and so, of course, is the William and Mary style itself. Thus the fashion of New York silver in the 1670s and 1680s was essentially the fashion which only came to Boston, via England, twenty years later. Thus it is that the leading New York silversmiths of the William and Mary style are the same as those active in the last two decades of the 17th

35 Teapot by Thomas Hammersley of New York, about 1760. This piece has an inscription dated 1762.

36 Sugar caster by Peter van Dyck, New York, about 1740.

37 Mug by Joseph Richardson Snr of Philadelphia. Mid 18th century.

35

 36

 37

38 Oval box by Samuel Vernon, Newport, Rhode Island, about 1725; trefid spoon by John Coney, Boston, about 1700; strainer by Benjamin Burt, Boston, about 1770.

39 Salver with the maker's mark of Lewis Fueter of New York. It was presented to a Captain Sowers in 1773. The New York Historical Society.

38

39

40 Caudle cup by Robert Sanderson of Boston, about 1680. It is interesting to compare the decoration and the caryatid handles with those on the Boelen bowl made in New York nearly twenty years later. The Henry Francis du Pont Winterthur Museum.

41 Miniature silver cup, only $1\frac{15}{16}$ inches high, by Caleb Shields of Baltimore, Massachusetts, about 1770.

42 Silver bowl by Jacob Boelen I of New York, about 1700. Boelen's mark on this piece has been overstruck by that of another New York silversmith, Simeon Soumaine, a rare occurrence which probably happened on resale.

40

41

42

43 Pair of silver sauceboats by Paul Revere
Jnr of Boston, Massachusetts, about 1785.
Engraved with the name Hays for Moses
Michael Hays, one of Revere's greatest patrons.

century, although a young maker who started his career at this time but who reached his peak during the Queen Anne period, was Peter van Dyck (1684–1751), who was probably a pupil of Bartholomew Le Roux.

Queen Anne silver, made in America between about 1715 and 1745, is characterised by its concern with shape and line, as was the furniture produced at the same time. Thus it is that in describing the silver of this period we may be anachronistic and apply the word 'functional' in its full 20th-century sense. The dignity of Queen Anne designs were to prove the underlying strength of all 18th-century English and American applied art.

During this period, certain famous forms made their appearance for the first time, notably the bullet or apple shape,
35 used almost exclusively for teapots, and the plain pear-shaped mugs known in America as cans. This was also the time when cut-card work, a beautifully simple type of applied decoration, was introduced, originating, it is thought, with French Huguenot silversmiths; it did appear on a few William and Mary pieces – we have mentioned the sugar box by Coney – but its greatest popularity was during the period under discussion.

There were unaccountable preferences for shapes amongst New York and Boston silversmiths, however. Thus the pear shape was favoured in New York and the bullet in Boston. It would seem that the Philadelphia makers followed the Boston preference, although the very small number of surviving examples make it difficult to reach any definite conclusion. It is worth remembering that the teapot itself was a comparatively new invention, the beverage having become only recently fashionable.

Another difference was the shape of tankards. Boston pieces tended to have a domed cover, while New York pieces retained the flat lid of previous styles, together with the inset coin. Philadelphia tankards, unlike the teapots, more closely approximate to those made in New York and one of the most outstanding pieces of early Philadelphia silver is the tankard made by Philip Syng Jnr (1703–89), made in about 1725–40, now at Yale. Other important Philadelphia makers of this
37 period include Joseph Richardson (1711–84), William Vilant and Joseph Ledell.

Nevertheless, if there are different preferences for shape, the underlying concern with formal values of the Queen Anne period brings New York and Boston silver closer together at this time than they had been in the previous forty or fifty years. Although New York silver still gives the impression, and it is only an impression, of greater richness, the magnificent structural qualities of the silver made by Simeon Sou-
44 maine of New York (1685–1750), so perfectly demonstrated in the justly famous sugar bowl of about 1740 at Yale, is very similar, if finer, to Boston examples by such makers as Jacob Hurd (1703–58) and Paul Revere Snr (1702–54).

The second half of the 18th century sees the development of a far more ornate Rococo style. Aesthetic movements appear to run in cycles and thus the plain functionalism of the Queen Anne period may be seen as a reaction against the Baroque decoration of William and Mary silver, while late 18th-century Rococo is a similar reaction against the conspicuous lack of decoration of the Queen Anne silver style.

If a single individual may be said to dominate American silver, it is Paul Revere Jnr of Boston, silversmith, engraver 43 and patriot. His father Paul Revere Snr, a Huguenot, was born in France in 1702, came to Boston in about 1715 and was apprenticed to John Coney (it is interesting that the great Boston silversmiths all form a line to Hull and Sanderson, who taught Coney, who taught Revere Snr, who taught his brilliant son). Revere Snr was himself an accomplished silversmith who made some extremely fine silver in the style of Queen Anne.

Paul Jnr was born in 1734, was apprenticed to his father, and by the age of twenty-four, was sufficiently well-known to be commissioned to make a chalice for the Old South Church, Boston. He went on to make more church pieces than any of his contemporaries, although the amount of surviving ecclesiastical silver *in toto* from this period is extremely small when compared to previous times.

In 1760, Revere was received into St Andrew's Lodge and on January 3, 1761, started the first of his two day books, valuable, if maddeningly incomplete, records of his own activities and of the clients and other silversmiths with whom he dealt.

In 1768, Revere made what has become the most famous piece of American silver, The Rescinders' or Sons of Liberty Bowl, now in the Museum of Fine Arts, Boston. *The Boston Gazette* of August 8, 1768, remarks on this piece as follows:

'We hear that the week before last was finished, by Order and for the Use of the Gentlemen belonging to the Insurance Office kept by Mr Nathanial Barber, at the North End, an elegant silver BOWL, weighing forty-five Ounces, and holding forty-five Jills. One side is engraved with a handsome border – To the Memory of the glorious NINETY-TWO Members of the Honourable House of Representatives of the Massachusetts Bay, who, undaunted by the insolent Menaces of Villains in Power, and out of strict regard to Constituents, on the 30th of June 1768, voted NOT TO RESCIND – over which is the Cap of Liberty in an Oaken Crown. On the other Side, in a Circle adorned with Flowers, &c. is No. 45, WILKES AND LIBERTY, under which is General Warrants torn to Pieces. On the Top of the Cap of Liberty, and out of each Side, is a Standard, on one is MAGNA CHARTA, the other BILL OF RIGHTS – On Monday Evening last, the Gentlemen belonging to the Office made a genteel Entertainment and invited a Number of Gentlemen of Distinction in the Town, when 45 Loyal Toasts were drank, and the whole concluded with a new Song, the Chorus of which is, In Freedom we're born, and in Freedom we'll live, &c. . . .'

Revere is not mentioned in the above as the maker, nor does his bowl appear in his day book; nevertheless, his pellet mark is stamped onto the bottom of the bowl. It should be noted that the frequent reference to 45, capacity, weight, number of toasts, stem from the 45th number of John Wilke's Republican newspaper, as mentioned in the inscription on the bowl.

A silver design specifically connected with Revere is the plain pitcher, with a slightly bulbous body, plain ear-shaped handle and short spout, a shape adapted from Liverpool pottery pitchers. Until his death in 1818, Revere busied himself in many fields, from making false-teeth and spectacle frames, to founding a copper rolling mill. But it is as the greatest of all American silversmiths, one who combined sumptuous elegance with bold, simple forms, that he will be always remembered.

The second half of the 18th century, in the years immediately preceeding and following the Revolution, saw the highest achievements of American craftsmen. The merchant classes grew phenomenally in wealth as the vast untapped resources of America began to be realised for the first time. This period also saw Philadelphia rise to a pre-eminent position amongst American cities, her silversmiths for the first time making a major contribution. These included Edmund Milne (active about 1757–1813), Philip Hulbaert (active about 1750–64), Richard Humphreys (active about 1771–96) and Joseph Richardson (1711–84).

In New York, silver was dominated by two outstanding 32 craftsmen, the famous Myer Myers (active about 1760–70) and Daniel Christian Fueter (active about 1754–76). One of the characteristics of New York silver of this period, and of Myers' work in particular, is the frequent use of pierced Rococo scrolls. Rococo is a word derived from the ubiquitous shell motifs of this period; this and other decorations adapted from natural forms, were richly applied to the basic shapes made current during the Queen Anne period.

38 Together with Paul Revere, Benjamin Burt (1729–1815) and Daniel Henchman (1730–75) were fine Boston makers. In addition to the two great makers we have mentioned as being active in New York, other important silversmiths working in 39 that city included Lewis Fueter (active circa 1770–88), who was the son of Daniel Christian, Richard van Dyck (1717–70), son of Peter, and Elias Pelletreau (1726–1810).

The growth of the rich mercantile classes, who were after all, the silversmiths' main patrons, and the greatly increased population not only in New England but also far down the coast in Virginia, the Carolinas and Georgia, gave craftsmen of all kinds great new markets. Thus apart from New York, Boston and Philadelphia, important makers came from Salem (John Andrew 1747–91), Lancaster (Charles Hall 1742–83), Newport, Rhode Island (Jonathan Clarke about 1705–70) and numerous provincial centres throughout Connecticut, Maryland and Pennsylvania.

The early Republic witnessed that style which, in furniture, is called Federal. This was based upon the Classical motifs which appealed to a society which at least in spirit allied itself to the ancient, if over-idealised, democracies of Greece and Rome. America, of course, did not discover these styles for herself–they had begun appearing in England and France in the 1760s.

44 Porringer by Simeon Soumaine of New York, about 1735.

The years between the Revolution and the War of 1812 saw the rise of New York as the first city of America, eclipsing even Philadelphia in riches. Boston still had Paul Revere Jnr, who unquestionably made his finest pieces in the more elegant Neo-classic period; but apart from him, Boston, was for the first time, short of fine craftsmen, a situation from which she never recovered.

Neo-classical silver is a style of elongated spheres, fluting 47 and reeding. Many people find it slightly anaemic and it certainly requires a silversmith of great ability to raise it above the level of dull repetition. Revere in Boston definitely succeeded in producing pieces of marvellously refined elegance, and certain other makers may be singled out–Joseph Richardson Jnr of Philadelphia (1752–1831), Daniel van Voorhis and Gerrit Schank of New York, who were working in partnership in New York between 1791 and 1792, Simeon Bayley of New York (active about 1789–96), Ephraim Brasher of New York (1744–1810), William G. Forbes of New York (1751–1840), John and James Black of Philadelphia and Ebenezer Chittenden of New Haven, Connecticut (1726–1812).

Following the War of 1812, the Neo-classical style gave way to the full blown opulence of the Empire style, combining not 46 only the Neo-classical motifs of such designers as John Stuart Flaxman but also Egyptian and Eastern designs–sphinxes and the like. New York was firmly established as the leading city of America by this time, although the greatest Empire silver was produced in Philadelphia by such makers as Harvey Lewis (active 1811–28), Anthony Rasch (active 1807–25) and Simeon Chaudron (active 1798–1825), who had emigrated from France.

Nevertheless, the end of the second decade of the 19th cen-

45 Silver by Paul Revere Jnr. The ladle was made in about 1770, the other three pieces date from about 1785.

46 Massive late Neo-classical pitcher by John Tagee of New York, about 1810–20.

47 A silver tea caddy by James Black of Philadelphia, about 1800.

48 A copper tray and ginger jar, inlaid with silver, by the Gorham Company, New York, made in 1879 and 1880 respectively. Collection Michael Whiteway, London.

46

47

48

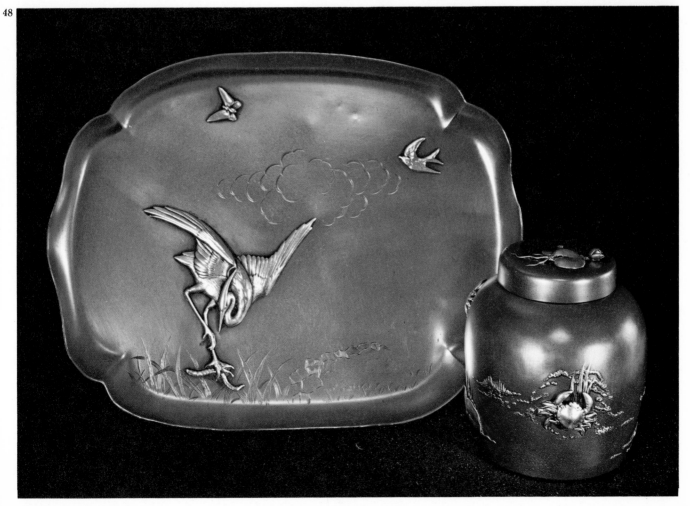

49 Pair of goblets by Bancroft Woodcock of Wilmington, Delaware. Late 18th century.

50 *left* Teapot by Gerardus Boyle, New York, about 1830. *right* Coffee pot in a mixed Greek Revival and Neo-Gothic style by the Gorham Company, New York, about 1870.

51 An Empire coffee pot, possibly by Garret Eoff, about 1830.

tury marked the beginning of the long decline of the individual craftsman and the rise of factory produced wares, culminating in the great companies like Tiffany's and the Gorham Manufacturing Company. Many of the products of these large companies were designed by specially commissioned artists of great talent, and a high proportion of it was splendidly made; but inevitably the quality of much silver, and of design, declined throughout the 19th century.

Of all the various styles which had influence upon the 19th-century silversmith, perhaps the most important, but as yet underrated, was the Japanese. Two American companies, Tiffany's and Gorham's, were not only among the first in the West to adapt Japanese metalwork designs but they were primarily responsible for spreading this style into Europe, and especially into England.

The Gorham Company was founded in Providence, Rhode Island, in 1831 by Jabez Gorham, although the major expansion of the company took place under his son John after Jabez's retirement in 1847. The New York sales office was opened in 1861, and further offices were opened in San Francisco and Chicago in 1878. In 1868, a London designer, Thomas Pairpont, came to work for the company and in 1887, Edward Holbrook, the fourth president of Gorham's, brought over another English designer, William J. Codman. It was the latter who was responsible for those sinuously eccentric pieces produced by Gorham called Martélé, which were marketed between 1890 and 1910.

Charles Lewis Tiffany (1812–1902) founded Tiffany's in 1834 in New York and started manufacturing jewellery in 1848. In 1868, Tiffany's became incorporated with the company founded by John C. Moore, and John's son Edward, a keen collector of Oriental art, became the first president of the new organisation. In the same year, Tiffany's opened a branch in London's Regent Street, where, six years later, Arthur Lazenby Liberty was to open his famous store.

Both the Gorham Company and Tiffany's began to produce inlaid and chased Japanese-style metalwork at around this time which was almost certainly fashioned, at least in part, by Japanese metalworkers, who had little employment in their own country following the Imperial ban on wearing swords promulgated in 1876. Indeed, in the Paris Exhibition of 1878, Tiffany's won a gold medal for their highly ornate pieces in the Japanese style, pieces which may however, have been designed by an Englishman called Christopher Dresser, a designer of incredible brilliance whose position in the history of 19th-century aesthetics is only now beginning to be appreciated.

It may, however, be safely said that Tiffany's and Gorham's, with their pioneering of Japanese designs, influenced English silversmiths, thus reversing the roles of the past two hundred years. Gorham's extremely beautiful copper pieces, with inlaid gold, silver, brass and lead decorations, and often lacquered, were exceptionally popular in Europe, as demonstrated by the large number of examples in English collections.

19th-century America witnessed an expansion in power and wealth unparalleled in the history of civilisation; the discovery of gold and silver, and the opening up of the vast expanses of the West, showed the world what a nation had come into being. More efficient methods of manufacturing electroplate were engendered by the two firms of Reed & Barton of Taunton, Massachusetts, founded in 1840, and the Meriden Britannia Company of Connecticut, founded in 1852. Apart from these, and of course Tiffany's and Gorham's, other great companies included Ball, Tompkins & Black of New York (from 1851 called Ball, Black & Company, and from 1876 Black, Starr & Frost) and Shreve Brothers of San Francisco.

If any pieces may be said, in their ostentatious vulgarity, to sum up the boisterous strivings of the Gilded Age, they are the Magnolia Vase, designed by John T. Curran for Tiffany's stand at the World's Columbian Exhibition of 1893 and the incredible gold Adam's vase, studded with semi-precious stones, executed by Tiffany's from designs by Paulding Farnham between 1893 and 1895. Both pieces, in the collection of the Metropolitan Museum of Art, New York, exhibit a complete lack of any aesthetic sensitivity, yet their sheer opulence, combined with a peerless technical mastery, makes them amongst the most amazing examples of American metalwork, once seen never forgotten.

52 Tea and coffee service by T. Fletcher and
T. Bailey, both of Philadelphia, about 1830.

55 Vase by Tiffany & Company, New York, about 1895. The stem of the vase is strongly influenced by Japanese designs, while the base is an adaptation of Chinese wooden stands.

56 Flagon by George B. Sharp of Philadelphia, about 1850.

55   56

54

GLASS

57 A fine ruby coloured footed bowl, containing a coin in the hollow bubble of the finial. Probably New England Glass Company, second quarter of the 19th century.

58 Early 19th-century South Jersey tradition footed vase containing a coin in the bubble of the stem.

The history of glass in America from the 18th to the 20th centuries centres around four great individuals, Caspar Wistar, William Henry 'Baron' Stiegel, John Frederick Amelung and Louis Comfort Tiffany. The first three were essentially working within a European idiom, whilst Tiffany proved to be an innovator of formidable genius whose products raised the level of American glass from national to international stature. It is no exaggeration to say that he is one of the greatest figures in the history of 19th-century art.

Glass is known to have been made in America in the 17th century, although, being then a less functional medium than wood, silver, pewter or ceramic, probably in small quantities. Six glasshouses are supposed to have operated and names like Evert Duycking of New Amsterdam and Johannes Smedes of the same city are associated with early glass-blowing. Apart from a few scattered fragments, however, which may originate from the two earliest American glasshouses, both located at Jamestown, Virginia, no certain piece of 17th-century glass from the New World has survived. The beginning of the documentary history of American glass may be located around the middle of the 18th century.

In American books on glass, a number of terms of reference are used to describe the chronology of the craft and have become standard. As we shall be using them throughout this chapter, it is as well to clarify them now:

Early South Jersey Glass blown in the South Jersey glasshouses which may be described as folk glass. It is free-blown and hand-decorated in a naive style and was probably blown from the left-overs from bottle-making, which glass-blowers used up in this way for their own purposes. The South Jersey tradition is an expression used to cover pieces made in the same style and in the same circumstances right up until the middle of the 19th century.

Pattern-moulded or 'Stiegel tradition' Refers to glass produced during the period of Henry Stiegel's second glasshouse at Manheim, 1769–1774. It does not refer specifically to glass made at this factory but to all roughly contemporary glass fashioned in the style associated with it.

Early Ohio glass This refers to glass in the Stiegel tradition which was blown at the Ohio glasshouses at Zanesville and Mantua between roughly 1815 and 1825.

Early historical and pictorial flasks Flasks produced between approximately 1820 and 1850 and bearing portraits mainly of famous American statesmen and soldiers.

Pressed pattern glass Tablewares made at Sandwich and other glasshouses in the period between 1820 and 1850.

Art glass Decorative and unusual glass associated with a number of individual craftsmen and glasshouses from about 1875 onwards. The greatest name is that of Louis Comfort Tiffany.

A number of other descriptions are used to cover the manufacturing processes or appearance of specific types of glass but these will be explained as they occur.

The earliest American glass of the South Jersey type is generally blown of natural glass, employing the range of colours produced by the presence of varying quantities of minerals. Such colours are restricted to a range of greens, yellows and browns. Soda or potash was the principal alkaline base. Later glass in the South Jersey tradition was often artificially coloured, usually in blue but in rare cases, in red or opaque white.

It is in examining the Early South Jersey glass, and the tradition to which it gave rise, that we encounter the first great name in the history of American glass, Caspar Wistar, who founded the glasshouse in Salem County, New Jersey, in 1739, which was to continue operations until 1780. Wistar himself had no practical qualifications for starting a glass factory – he is described in the initial agreement dated December 7, 1738, as a 'brass-button maker' – and it must have taken considerable courage on his part since he had to defy openly the ban imposed by the British Government on glass-manufacturing in the colonies. In the agreement, however, four 'experts in glass-making' are listed: John William Wentzell, Caspar Halter, John Martin Halton and Simon Kreismeier, all of whom probably came from Germany.

The main products of this enterprise, as of all early American glasshouses, was bottle and window glass, but the pieces with which we are concerned are the free-blown bowls, dishes, jugs, pitchers and other practical wares which the blowers fashioned out of the left-overs for their own personal use and not on a commercial scale.

George and Helen McKearin, in their monumental study *American Glass*, remark that 'it is in these individual or off-hand free-blown pieces, blown in many bottle and window-glass houses and not in factories specialising in table and ornamental wares for the fashionable market, that the South Jersey tradition is embodied. It is for these reasons that the glass . . . has the intangible but distinctive characteristics of individuality and the naiveté and peasant quality associated with folk art. In fact it has been called American folk art in glass.'

Early pieces of the South Jersey type are characterised by the bold swirls of their applied decoration, which often became standardised in motif, the most famous and original being the so-called 'lily-pad'. In the 19th century, South Jersey tradition pieces, as well as those made by commercial tableware factories, employed the 'looping and dragging' decoration of contrasting colours which is perhaps best illustrated in Europe by the products of the Nailsea factory. In America, however, it was not a common form of decoration and was mainly used in South Jersey itself. Some early sugar bowls have finials tooled into the shape of a bird, these being known as swan finials.

The South Jersey tradition spread through all the settled areas and certain differences in colour help towards establishing in which particular region a piece was made. The majority of examples from South Jersey itself are pale aquamarine, ranging through the green-yellow spectrum. Far more rare colours are blue and amber. South Jersey pieces from New York are usually aquamarine also, but of a far more brilliant, bluish, shade. Light blue was used only from about 1840 onwards and a few New York pieces in amber, and olivy greens and yellows are known.

In contrast to pieces from New York and New Jersey, New England glass in this tradition is rarely found in aquamarine, amber and olive-green being the most frequently used colours. Pieces from the west, while employing the complete range of colours found on South Jersey, New York and New England pieces, are distinguishable by their plainness; they rarely employ the ornate shapes associated with the main centres.

Before moving on to discuss the second great tradition in American glass, we should mention the other outstanding South Jersey factory, that founded by the two Stanger brothers between 1780 and 1781 at Glassboro, Gloucester County. Both brothers were probably apprenticed to Wistar, and one of them, Jacob, certainly was. He absconded in April, 1770, in which month, Richard Wistar, son of Caspar, offered a reward for his return. The Stanger family, and the companies they founded, are influential in the history of American glass. The original Glassboro factory passed through several hands, operated under various names but did not cease production until 1918, while the Harmony Glass Works, founded by the Stangers in 1813, produced fine glass for many years.

From the early beginnings of the two New Jersey glasshouses, the traditions they established spread through America. The majority of the South Jersey tradition pieces known today date from the 19th century and few can be assigned to any particular factory. In addition, no pieces can certainly be attributed to either Wistar or the first Glassboro factory, although it is a reasonable hypothesis that the few surviving 18th-century pieces of this type were made by either one or the other of them.

The second great tradition in American glass is that named after William Henry 'Baron' Stiegel. He was born in Cologne, Germany on May 13, 1729 and landed in Philadelphia on August 31, 1750. Cologne was in fact one of the major glass-producing centres of Europe so it is not surprising that in his adopted country Stiegel should seek to establish a craft which must have been familiar to him.

His creative life was short; his first glasshouse at Elizabeth Furnace started production on September 18, 1763 and his third venture, at Manheim, ceased operations in 1774. The last entry in Stiegel's copious daybooks, now preserved by the Historical Society of Pennsylvania, reads 'Glass House shut down', a sad testimonial to a man whose creative energy so greatly enriched the applied arts of America.

As with silver, ceramics and, to a lesser extent, furniture, the rich American merchant class of this period still favoured imported European goods, not only because they were, in general, of higher quality but also because they reflected

64

58

6

social prestige upon their owners. It is usually easy to distinguish European from American products, but with glass, the situation is still slightly confused. Most of the major American glasshouses of this time employed European, mainly German, workmen, who carried on the traditions of their native country virtually unchanged and handed them on to their apprentices.

In Stiegel's case, the situation is further complicated; not only are his pieces never signed but he followed European styles so closely and with such a high degree of technical ability, that it still requires a very advanced 'eye' and, hopefully, a fairly accurate history for a given piece, to be absolutely certain about its origins. Modern scientific methods of analysis have helped considerably, but the art of authenticating American glass is still a very specialised activity.

As we have said, most of the employees of American glasshouses were Germans, and Stiegel's ventures do not seem to have been exceptions. Amongst the craftsmen at Elizabeth Furnace were Christian Nasel, Martin Grenier, Benjamin Misky, Daniel M. Daniel, Michael Griesbach, George Glass, Mathias Hoffart, Michael Miller and Anton Walder. It is also probable that Stiegel's factories were the first to produce enamelled glass in America, since three of his workmen, Joseph Welch, Sebastian Witmer and Martin Yetters are known to have been enamelers, and Stiegel advertised enameled pieces for sale between 1772 and 1773.

The principal products of all three of Stiegel's glasshouses were almost certainly bottles and there is nothing particularly significant about the pieces made either at the Elizabeth Furnace factory or the first Manheim glassworks, which started production in 1765. It is obvious, however, that Stiegel was not daunted by the various economic crises through which these initial ventures passed since in 1768, he started building a far more elaborate factory which between 1769 and 1774, produced a large range of glass in great quantity and of a hitherto unapproached standard. It could be truthfully said that the products of Stiegel's second Manheim works equalled any that were being produced in Europe.

He obviously overestimated his market, however, or rather he underestimated the colonial prejudice against domestic products at this time, since this splendidly extrovert figure ended his career in bankruptcy. Like so many great craftsmen, he was before his time; in the patriotic fervour of the post-Revolutionary period, he would doubtless have enjoyed great financial success.

Although the principal products of this last great venture were still probably bottles, it is the so-called flint glass (or clear glass of a lead base) tableware for which it is most justly famous. It is not certain if Stiegel was the first manufacturer to produce clear lead glass in America. The contemporaneous Philadelphia Glass Works almost certainly produced it as did the Glasshouse Company of New York City. This latter company was founded in 1752 and ceased production in 1767 – therefore it had had fifteen years of production before Stiegel's third factory had been built. Yet no pieces have survived

which can with certainty be attributed to it. The one piece of evidence we do have which suggests that sophisticated lead glass of the Stiegel type was produced there is the fact that in the list of inevitably German employees of this factory, we find the name Johan Martin Grenier, who, it seems certain, is the same Martin Grenier we have noted above as being an employee of Stiegel.

The McKearins summarise the main difference between the Stiegel tradition and the South Jersey tradition as follows: 'Whereas the South Jersey represents individual expression of the art of glass-blowing, the Stiegel might be said to epitomise skills standardised to conform to the commercial requirements for table and ornamental wares.'

Apart from Stiegel's engraved and enameled pieces, very **61** few of which have survived, his main contribution was the introduction of pattern-moulded decoration, a technique widely employed in the Bristol factories in England. Apart from ribbing and fluting, the main pattern-moulded designs are geometric rows of diamonds, hexagons etc. Stiegel **59** intentionally copied English glass as closely as possible, so that it is, as we have said, extremely difficult to tell native and imported pieces apart.

Before discussing the glass of John Frederick Amelung, we should, perhaps, take a wider look at Stiegel's influence. After the collapse of his last company, his workmen spread throughout the western states, producing glass of a higher quality than the established South Jersey type. Ohio is officially associated with superbly coloured pattern-moulded bottles and flasks which are now amongst the most keenly collected types of American glass. It is also probable that Stiegel's workmen were employed at the Philadelphia Glass Works, which, however, only survived Stiegel's last venture by three years, at the Schuykill Glass Works (1780–86) of Robert Morris and John Nicholson, at the Baltimore Glass Works and at the New Bremen Glass Works of Amelung himself.

Of all these factories, the most important, apart from Amelung's, was the Philadelphia Glass Works, established in 1771 by Robert Towers and Joseph Leacock. No certainly authenticated pieces have survived but it is obvious from contemporary evidence that this was a reasonably successful concern producing a wide range of fine lead glass. In common with Stiegel, they attempted, and doubtless succeeded, to produce glass of equal quality to imported English wares.

Also, like Stiegel, the Philadelphia Glass Works attempted to drum up popular support. In the *Pennsylvania Packet* of March 22, 1773, an air of desperation creeps into their appeal, possibly aggravated by the fact that the advertisers were aware of Stiegel's impending bankruptcy and feared for the same fate themselves: 'It is . . . hoped that the inhabitants of these provinces, and of this city in particular, will, in purchasing, give the preference to Goods manufactured by their fellow citizens, whereby they may be likely to receive again the money they expend, which it is in vain to expect when sent beyond the seas.' This appeal, and the lotteries started by both

59 Five items of Stiegel pattern-moulded glass.
The perfume bottle or flask in the centre
has the so-called 'quilted diamond' pattern,
the only known pattern which has been
positively identified as originating with Stiegel.

Stiegel and the Philadelphia Glass Works to raise ready cash, were obviously not successful. Stiegel himself retired bankrupt in 1774 and the latter company was put up for sale in 1777.

We have said that the wares produced by the major factories at this time were, considering the handicaps under which they were working, of extraordinary variety. Just how much they were capable of making is evidenced by a Philadelphia Glass Works advertisement of 1775, in which are offered:

'Decanters from one gallon to half a pint; wine glasses of various sorts; tumblers of all sizes, bottles for cases &c. flint or other beer glasses; basons, cans of all sizes, candlesticks and sockets, confectioner glasses, cyder glasses, canisters, bitter bottles, bird cisterns and boxes, candle shades, cruets and casters, chimney arms, cream pots, cupping glasses, dishes for sallad, &c. electric globes and cylinders, garter bells, hour glasses, ink cups, lamps for halls, streets, chambers, shops, weavers &c. mortars and pestles, nipple shells and pipes, pyramids, pipes for tobacco, salvers of various sizes, salt cellars, sugar dishes, spice bottles, urinals, wine and water glasses, goblets, Jelly glasses, jeweler's glasses, mustard pots, proof bottles, pocket bottles, syllabub glasses, sweet meat ditto, salt linings, smelling bottles, tubes for thermometers &c. Phials of all sizes &c.'

The Philadelphia Glass Works, it is worth adding, found a purchaser and after passing through several hands, was acquired in the 19th century by the famous Thomas W. Dyott, who changed its name to the Dyotville Glass Works, which produced some of the most famous American bottles and flasks. In the last quarter of the 18th century, two other one-time Stiegel employees, Felix Farrer, who went into partnership with George Bakeoven in 1777, and Lazarus Isaac, started independent businesses in Philadelphia, the latter advertising himself as a glass-engraver.

John Frederick Amelung established his glasshouse at New Bremen, Frederick County, Maryland, in 1784, having been born in Bremen, Germany. Like Stiegel, his career was short, the factory ceasing production in 1795, but he too occupies a place at the forefront of glass-manufacturing in America, and may be considered as one of the outstanding American 18th-century craftsmen.

Working in the same tradition as Stiegel, Amelung's products are far more sophisticated. Glass was certainly engraved at Stiegel's factory but the pieces which are attributed to him are extremely crude when compared to Amelung's, whose wheel-engraved pieces are infinitely 'superior to any ever produced in America', to quote Mr Boudinot during the Congressional debate in 1790 concerning Amelung's request for a loan. Indeed, so high is the quality of his best pieces that when in 1928, the celebrated Amelung Pokal, or covered goblet, was discovered in, of all places, Bremen, Germany, it was sometime before scholars would believe the engraved inscription, 'New Bremen Glassmanufactury/1788/North America State of Maryland', so far in advance was it of any then known American glass.

Since that time, a small group of superbly decorated, and dated, pieces have come to light. Apart from the Pokal, the Metropolitan owns another piece dated 1791, while the Corning Museum of Glass's magnificent 'Tobias and the Angel' 63 covered tumbler is dated 1788 and is dedicated to a member of the Amelung family. In the Winterthur Collection is another tall covered tumbler made for Charles Ghequiere and dated June 20, 1788 and in the Yale University Art Gallery, Boston, there is an uncovered tumbler dated '23 Jan 1789' and signed 'John Fr. Amelung & Company'. This group, it should be noted, includes the only signed and dated pieces of 18th-century American glass to have survived and is valuable testimony to the splendid achievements of the colonial glassmaker.

By 1790, Amelung had two glasshouses in production at New Bremen and had invested something like £23,000 in the ventures, a sum equal in terms of the present purchasing power of money to about £500,000 or $1,250,000. Most of the original money had come from investors in Germany, and the Metropolitan Pokal may have been sent by Amelung to his native city to satisfy his backers as to his abilities. They should have been assured, although the fact that in 1790 Amelung had to apply for a loan to Congress shows that foreign capital was not forthcoming in sufficient quantity. Even granted Amelung's high standards, he was still unable to break the back of both European and domestic competition and his factories went into liquidation in 1795.

Apart from the engraved goblets and tumblers mentioned above, which are probably the most valuable examples of American glass, Amelung certainly produced wine glasses as did both Stiegel and the Philadelphia Glass Works. In trying to determine whether wine glasses found in American loca-

tions were European or American, the McKearins propounded a hypothesis which may be considered the rule of thumb. They pointed out that most 18th-century wine glasses found in the United States were of clear soda-lime glass in either English or Irish styles. Yet most English or Irish glass of the period is lead glass. Although Continental wines were frequently made of soda-lime glass, they may be easily distinguished stylistically. Thus, if given an 18th-century soda-lime wine glass in an English or Irish style, it is very probably American.

A number of other late 18th-century glasshouses producing glass of the Stiegel-Amelung type are important to the student. In the west, the first flint glasshouse was started by Albert Galatin at New Geneva, Pennsylvania, in 1797. Several of his workmen had been employed by Amelung, and these included members of the Kramer family, one of whom, Baltazar, had also worked for Stiegel at Manheim.

Another glasshouse was built by the Kramers across the river at Greensboro in 1807 which produced identical glass and the products of both factories, which are either free-blown from bottle glass in the South Jersey tradition, or pattern-moulded, are known under the generic name of Galatin-Kramer glass. It seems likely that the main activity of both houses was the manufacture of bottles and windows but the several surviving examples of tableware show that this was an important part of their output. They are usually of good quality and are further evidence of the spreading Stiegel-Amelung tradition.

Other significant glasshouses include the Pitkin Glass Works located at Manchester, Connecticut (1783–about 1830), which is famous for its long-necked Chestnut or Ludlow bottles and other bottles of various shapes, the Albany Glass-

works, near Albany, New York, which was founded in 1785, collapsed in 1789 and restarted under different ownership in 1792. This lasted into the 19th century but is not to be confused with a second, and entirely unconnected Albany Glassworks, which was in production during the 1820s. The Temple Glasshouse, New Hampshire, and the Boston Crown Glass Company, Boston, were both founded by Robert Hewes, the former in 1780 and the latter in 1793. Neither was particularly outstanding and, like all the factories mentioned in this paragraph, produced mainly window glass and bottles. The Boston Crown Glass Company failed in 1803, was restarted in 1809 by another group but finally ceased production in 1829.

By the end of the 18th century, glass manufacturing was established in America, albeit on somewhat shaky grounds. Almost all glasshouses founded between 1750 and 1800 ended in bankruptcy after only a few years of life even though many of them were producing glass equal in quality to that imported from Europe.

During the first three decades of the 19th century, the industry grew enormously but the casualty rate still remained alarmingly high. Between 1800 and 1840, some 120 glass factories were in production, some only for a very few years. Between about 1810 and 1812, the industry flourished on a wave of patriotic fervour, but after the Treaty of Ghent in 1814, English manufacturers were quick to exploit the new market, and with their more efficient methods of production, their generally finer glass and their business acumen, were prepared to flood the American market with fine quality wares at cost and even below-cost prices to secure a monopoly. They succeeded in forcing many domestic firms into liquidation. Added to this, the social prestige attached to English wares,

60 A Dyottville Glassworks pictorial glass
flask of about 1880, showing General
Zachary Taylor on one side and George
Washington on the other.

61 Two very rare free-blown enameled tumblers dating from about 1770–74, perhaps made in Stiegel's second glassworks at Manheim, Pennsylvania. The Corning Museum of Glass, Corning, New York.

62 Free-blown bottle glass sugar bowl of the South Jersey type, from either Wistarburg or Glassboro. Last quarter of the 18th century. The Corning Museum of Glass, Corning, New York.

63 The celebrated 'Tobias and the Angel' engraved covered tumbler, dated 1788, made at the factory of John Frederick Amelung, New Bremen, Maryland. The Corning Museum of Glass, Corning, New York.

61

62

63

something which had crippled the great 18th-century makers, still existed, although only in the rich, middle-class, Eastern seaboard area. The Midwest was less sophisticated and discriminating, which accounts for the concentration of one-third of American glasshouses there. In his *Narrative of a Journey* published in London in 1818, Henry Bradshaw Fearon wrote: 'It is well to bear in mind that the demand for the articles of elegant luxury lies in the Western States! The inhabitants of Eastern America being still importers from the old country.' In the 1820s, the rapid growth of population and a protective tariff on imported goods, helped the domestic industry to grow, as did more efficient methods of manufacture, but in 1837, the economic slump caused a further setback, destroying some twenty-two glasshouses overnight.

One of the major innovations during the third decade of the 19th century was the invention of mechanically pressed glass, in which field America was the pioneer. (Hitherto, pattern-moulded glass of the Stiegel-type had been *blown* in moulds, with the small applied parts–handles, finials, etc.–formed in hand-operated presses.)

In 1825, John P. Bakewell of Bakewell & Company of Pittsburgh, obtained the first known patent for a crude form of mechanical press to make glass furniture nobs, while in 1827, Enoch Robinson of the New England Glass Company succeeded in making a mechanically pressed table salt. By 1830, the press had been made so efficient that it was standard equipment in most important factories. A popular type of mid 19th-century pressed table glass was the Lacy glass, made in a wide range of colours by all the major American glasshouses and so-called because of its resemblance to the patterns used in lace. It should not be forgotten, however, that the South Jersey tradition of free-blown glass continued well into the 19th century, indeed, as we have said before, most surviving South Jersey glass *is* 19th century.

Early mechanically pressed glass is crudely finished compared to hand-polished pieces blown in a pattern mould. Like the other great innovation in glass manufacturing during the 1820s, blown three-mould, it closely follows the designs and patterns of English and Irish cut glass and was doubtless intended as an inexpensive substitute.

Blown three-mould, like Stiegel's earlier pattern-moulded glass, was blown in a press, which in this case was in three separate parts hinged together, thus accomodating more ornate and sizeable pieces. It was given various names when first separately identified one of which was, inevitably, 'Stiegel', although Stiegel himself is now known never to have used this method. It is superior to mechanically pressed glass of the type mentioned above and, while employing many of the English and Irish cut glass designs, it invented many of its own which are considered amongst the first original American contributions to glass patterns. These patterns have been classified under three general stylistic headings, Arch, Baroque and Geometric, of which the last named is the most common.

Apart from Tiffany at the end of the period we are now

covering, there were two very important American glasshouses, the Bakewell Factory at Pittsburgh and the Boston & Sandwich Glass Company.

Bakewell & Company, afterwards called Bakewell & Page, Bakewell, Page & Bakewell (1824–36), and Bakewell, Pears & Company (1836–81), was founded in Pittsburgh in 1808. One of their main claims to fame is that they were the first manufacturers of cut glass in the United States, this being supervised by one of their craftsmen, Peter Eichbaum, who is credited with cutting the first American crystal glass chandelier. Mrs Anne Royall in her book on Pennsylvania published in Washington in 1829, remarked: 'The glass of Pittsburgh and the parts adjacent, is known and sold from Maine to New Orleans. Even in Mexico they quaff their beverage from the beautiful white flint of Messrs Bakewell, Page & Bakewell.'

The Boston & Sandwich Glass Company was the main part of the glass empire created by America's leading industrial entrepreneur in this field, the ubiquitous Deming Jarves of Boston. The son of a successful cabinetmaker, John Jackson Jarves, Deming served as a clerk with the Boston Porcelain & Glass Manufacturing Company, which in 1837, he and a group of associates bought and renamed the New England Glass Company, with which Jarves was associated for some seven years.

In 1825, he started his own Sandwich Manufacturing Company, which was renamed the Boston & Sandwich Glass Company the following year. Over the next few years, this factory became extraordinarily successful and was unquestionably the greatest American glasshouse of the first half of the 19th century. Of its wares, the McKearins have written: 'Its pressed Lacy tablewares and salts, not only in clear but in coloured glass, were rarely equalled and never excelled by any other manufacturer in America.' The same may be said of their flint glass pressed lamps, vases and candlesticks and indeed the whole range of glass tableware which they produced.

In 1858, Jarves left the firm he had founded but still as energetic as ever, immediately founded another factory, the Cape Cod Glass Works, which specialised in types of glass we would now describe as art glass–the white, opaque Sandwich Alabaster or the richly coloured Peachblow.

One other of Jarves' establishments which should not be allowed to pass without mention is the Mount Washington Glass Works which he started for his son George D. Jarves in 1837. While producing fine quality glass, the main interest of this works to the student of the history of American glass is that William L. Libbey received his training there and purchased the factory in 1869, selling out the following year and becoming an agent for the other factory started by Deming Jarves, the New England Glass Works. This also was purchased by Libbey, in 1880, who took his son Edward into partnership. After his father's death in 1883, Edward changed the factory's name to the Libbey Glass Company which he continued to operate until 1890. The Mount Washington

Glass Works, as we shall see later, also made some fine art glass.

The period between roughly 1840 and 1890 witnessed the massive production of pictorial flasks and bottles which are now so popular with collectors. Bottles were the staple products of most American glasshouses from the 17th century onwards, the earliest known example thought by some scholars to be American being the famous piece bearing the name 'N/GREEN' and the date 1724. That they were important items of barter is demonstrated by their discovery in many Indian graves, especially in Alabama, although it is doubtful if any of these is of colonial manufacture. It is known, however, that Caspar Wistar's factory produced bottles in the first half of the 18th century, these being the standard 'black' glass products of the period.

During the mid 19th century, fine pictorial glass flasks began to be produced, perhaps the finest and most splendidly coloured examples of which were made by the Dyottville Glass Works of Philadelphia and the Lockport Glass Works, at Lockport New York. These are usually ornamented with portraits of American statesmen and soldiers: George Washington, 'Father of his Country', the never-surrendering General Zachary Taylor, known as 'Old Rough and Ready', Henry Clay, Andrew Jackson, General Lafayette, Benjamin Franklin, John Adams, William Henry Harrison, DeWitt Clinton, progenitor of the Erie Canal or 'Clinton's Ditch' as it was derisorily known. Louis Kossuth, leader of the Hungarian Revolution of 1848–50, appealed to the republican sentiments of the newly independent America, and his stay in the United States between 1851 and 1852 was marked by several contemporaneously made flasks bearing his portrait. Jenny Lind, the Swedish nightingale, was a great success when brought to America by the impressario P. T. Barnum in 1850, and amongst the plethora of souvenirs produced to coincide with her tour, the flasks bearing her portrait are the only ones which have enduring interest. Other decorative motifs on flasks include sheaves of wheat, the American flag and the Federal eagle, the bust of Columbia, emblematic of national liberty, cornucopias and various emblems connected with masonry.

Before moving on to art glass, we should look briefly at the manufacture of paperweights in America. In this field, the influence of France was supreme, with its three great factories of St Louis, Clichy and Baccarat. The finest American examples, made by the New England Glass Company, the Boston & Sandwich Glass Company and at the factory established by John L. Gilliland in Brooklyn, New York, certainly do not equal the French paperweights, although they are of very good quality.

The Sandwich paperweights are of similar design to the French examples, which is not surprising in view of the fact that the leading craftsman engaged upon their manufacture was Nicolas Lutz, who had been brought over from the St Louis factory in France; millefiori, bouquet and fruit and flower weights were the main products. The weights made by the New England Glass Company were very similar and their leading craftsman, François Pierre, had worked at the Baccarat factory. Gilliland's weights are of the millefiori type and are of good quality, whilst outstanding pieces were made at the Mount Washington Glass Works. A characteristically American variety of paperweight was made by Whitall, Tatum & Company's Millville Works in New Jersey. Designs included the popular Millville lily, animals, and hunting scenes. Between 1905 and 1912, Ralph Barber produced the beautiful Millville rose weights.

American art glass is one of the greatest individual attainments of the applied arts in the United States; it produced one outstanding figure, Louis Comfort Tiffany, son of Charles Lewis Tiffany, founder of the famous store, and, like the silver produced by his father, Louis Comfort's glass was equal, if not superior, to any that was being produced in Europe. Only the finest achievements of the Frenchman Emil Gallé may be compared to Tiffany's products.

If Tiffany was the greatest manufacturer, other factories were producing important and unusual glass at the same time. The main two were houses we have met before, the New England Glass Company and its successor firm, the Libbey Glass Company, and the Mount Washington Glass Works, both of which were founded by Deming Jarves in the early 19th century.

The most common type of early art glass was Amberina, a clear yellow glass shading to red (or clear red shading to yellow, called Reverse Amberina). This was made by most glass manufactories in England as well as in America. A particular variety, called Plated Amberina, which has an opalescent glass lining and protruding vertical ribs, was made exclusively by the New England Glass Company from 1886.

The other extremely popular type of art glass was the so-called Peachblow, named after, and inspired by, a Chinese peach-bloom porcelain vase sold by Mrs Morgan at auction in New York in 1886 for the sensational price of $18,000. The basic colour scheme of Peachblow glass is white shading to a deep rich pink, although colour variations identify the various factories in which it was made. Thus the scheme we have described is typical of the New England Glass Company, while Mount Washington examples are blue-white shading to purple-pink, and, on some rare pieces, enameled with flowers. The Boston & Sandwich Glass Company's examples are, in fact, a monochrome dull pink, while those made by Hobbs, Brocunier & Company of Wheeling, West Virginia, are gold-yellow shading to orange-red. Glass copies of the Morgan vase itself were made, complete with stand, in the form of five dragons, in a contrasting glass.

Of the types of art glass originating with the Mount Washington Factory, the one they named Burmese in 1885 is probably the most internationally famous. In fact, it is a kind of Peachblow, or rather Peachblow is a kind of Burmese, being yellow shading to salmon pink. It was made under licence in England by Thomas Webb & Sons, although always with an acid, matt finish. American pieces may be either matt or glossy. Washington also made mother-of-pearl glass, and in

71

60

64 Free-blown bottle glass pitcher with lily-pad decoration, South Jersey type glass, 1840–60. The Corning Museum of Glass, Corning, New York.

65 Tiffany Wisteria glass and bronze lamp.

66 Three pieces of pressed Lacy glass, a compote, covered bowl and a cake plate. Probably made by the Boston & Sandwich Glass Company of Sandwich, Massachusetts, between 1830 and 1845. The Corning Museum of Glass, Corning, New York.

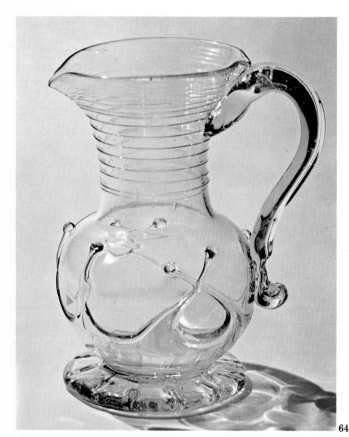

64

65

66

67 A selection of five superb Tiffany Favrile
glass vases. The tall piece in the centre is of
the 'goose-neck' shape derived from Persian glass.

68 Two blown three-mould pitchers in cobalt blue and clear glass, probably by the Boston & Sandwich Glass Company, about 1830. **69** Cut glass compote attributed to Bakewell, Page & Bakewell of Pittsburgh, about 1825. **70** Pair of Sandwich glass fluid lamps in the 'Sandwich Star' pattern. About 1840–50.

71 Rare pink rose paperweight by the Mount Washington Glass Company, about 1850.

72 Superb Tiffany Favrile glass Peacock vase with silver-gilt Fabergé mounts, workmaster Johan Viktor Arne.

1890, two exclusive types were introduced, Crown Milano, predominantly a beige-yellow colour with floral decoration, and Royal Flemish, with contrasting beige and tan panels and shapes and decorative motifs loosely inspired by Islamic glass and metalwork.

Types of glass exclusive to the New England Glass Company were the self-descriptive green opaque, first made in 1887, Agata, a type of Peachblow with mottled gold over-decoration, and the etched white-yellow Pomona glass.

Louis Comfort Tiffany started manufacturing glass in 1879 and the factory founded by him lasted until 1938, five years after his death. Until 1902, when the company was officially named Tiffany Studios, it was given a variety of names which were, in chronological order, as follows: 1879–85 Louis C. Tiffany & Company, Associated Artists; 1885–92 Tiffany Glass Company; 1892–1900 Tiffany Glass & Decorating Company; 1900–02 Allied Artists Company. In 1894, Tiffany patented the word 'Favrile', from the old English word 'fabrile', mean- **67,72** ing 'to fashion by hand', to describe all the pieces, including enamels, ceramics and glass made under his personal supervision, a kind of brand name which has now come to be applied almost exclusively to the glass.

Ray and Lee Grover, in their definitive book, *Art Glass Nouveau*, differentiate thirteen separate types of Tiffany glass, which are monochrome irridescent pieces, irridescent pieces with millefiori decoration, paperweight pieces, Cypriote glass (made to simulate the irridescent effects found upon buried Roman glass), Lava glass (literally glass resembling molten lava), Agate and marbleised glass, Cameo glass, Intaglio glass, Peacock Feather, Diatreta (a type of monochrome glass to which heavy gold glass latticework is applied), and the swirled bottle glass used in the making of lamps and stained-glass windows.

Of the vases, and similar pieces, by far the most highly rated are the paperweight type. This glass, as its name implies, is a heavy glass in which the decorative motifs appear suspended in the middle, as in paperweights. Glass and bronze lamps and stained-glass panels are also much sought after, with the magnificent wisteria lamp being the most popular and most **65** expensive (good examples now cost about £7,000 or $17,500).

Tiffany's influence was all-pervasive in America. The Quezal Art Glass & Decorating Company of Brooklyn, New York, was founded by one of Tiffany's ex-workmen, Martin Bach, at the turn of the century, and produced good quality irridescent pieces very similar to Tiffany's, as did W. S. Blake at the Union Art Glass Company–he named his glass Kew Blas, an anagram of his initials and surname.

The Steuben Glass Works was founded in 1903 by T. G. Hawkes and Frederick Carder, was sold to the Corning Glass Works in 1918, and continued to make fine art glass up until the mid 1930s. They produced superb, irridescent pieces simi- **73** lar to Tiffany's, as well as Jade glass, similar in appearance to that stone, Ivrene, a beautiful ivory-white opaque glass, and the white streaked and bubbled glasses called Clutha and Cintra.

73 A group of blue Aurene iridescent glass
vases by the Steuben Glass Works, Corning,
New York, about 1905. The Corning Museum
of Glass, Corning, New York.

CERAMICS

74 Pennsylvania sgraffito dish dated
January 29, 1772.

American ceramics may be divided into four main groups: folk pottery, porcelain, commercial pottery and art pottery. The era of the folk potter covers the first two hundred years of the New World's existence, but began to wane with the increased industrialisation of the mid 19th century. Within folk pottery, there are two distinct traditions – earthenware and stoneware.

Porcelain first began to be manufactured in the United States in the 1820s but never with great success. Only a few manufacturers succeeded in making worthwhile pieces and it is one of the most negligible of the applied arts in America.

The commercial pottery movement began in the 1820s and continued throughout the century. Many manufacturers also experimented with porcelain, but it was with fine stoneware and earthenware that they were primarily concerned and at which they were most successful. The real impetus came in the 1850s with the great international exhibitions, when American manufacturers strove to emulate the European styles as well as producing pieces on the necessary industrial scale.

The making of art pottery, as in England, increased steadily from the late 1870s and reached great heights with the products of the Rookwood Pottery Factory in the 1880s and 1890s. Unlike England, the impetus had gone by the end of the first decade of the 20th century.

Of these four very separate groups, the American folk pottery tradition stands out as by far the most interesting and rewarding. The finest redware with its rich colour and rough, but effective, glazes, is perhaps the nearest Western society has come to equalling the great pottery of China and Japan. Folk pottery was essentially simple and functional and the makers were often men of strictly limited ability. However, within the narrow range of their capabilities, they created, in many cases, great works of art of enduring beauty and importance.

Earthenware was produced in America from the beginning. We know of at least three potters arriving in 1635, Philip Drinker at Charlestown, Massachusetts and William Vincent and John Pride who settled at Salem. Not surprisingly, the major source of folk pottery has been New England – Connecticut, Massachusetts and New Hampshire – while a distinctive type of richly decorated pottery was produced in Pennsylvania by the German settlers, or Pennsylvania **75** 'Dutch' as they are inaccurately called ('Dutch' being a corruption of *Deutsch*) who were 18th-century emigrants from the Palatinate, a small German state.

The basic colours of earthenware come from impurities in the clay, which react when fired. Thus the most common type, redware, is caused by iron oxide, green is from copper oxide and manganese gives various shades of yellow, brown, and black, depending upon the quantity.

The earliest New England earthenware was formed into very simple functional shapes, with decoration kept to a minimum, usually only finger impressions or incised lines made with a stick. The glaze too was extremely basic, just a thin coating of interior lead-glaze. In the 18th century, more sophisticated glazes were introduced including the standard liquid glaze compounded of galena, litharge (red lead), sand and clay. Other glazes, like the basic colours of clay, were based upon metallic oxides; green glazes and slips come from copper and were the most expensive to produce, thus they are rarely found today. The yellow antimony oxide slips were most popular in Pennsylvania, while blue was obtained from cobalt.

Most early pottery is unmarked. In general, the potter considered himself an essential artisan producing necessary goods with little or no pretensions to aesthetic significance; thus he saw no reason to mark his pieces, as did potters of later generations. A further reason may be that English ceramics were greatly preferred to the domestic product and unscrupulous store owners would not hesitate to pass off American pottery as English to their status-conscious customers.

The pottery tradition of the Pennsylvania 'Dutch' was similar to that which they had practised in their own country. Their pieces are frequently decorated with hunting scenes, birds, animals and plants, many of which had a religious significance. Thus a deer would immediately bring to mind the sentiment expressed in William Cowper's hymn 'As pants the hart for cooling streams . . .' A tree was, of course, symbolic of the Tree of Life and the tulip suggested humility. A peculiarly haughty bird often found on plates and dishes from Pennsylvania is the 'Gaudy Bird of Paradise' who, in the Song of Solomon, 'feeds among lilies'.

One of the most famous techniques, imported directly from Europe, was sgraffito, in which the design is created by scratching through the outer glaze to expose the colour of the clay beneath (the word is derived from the Italian *sgraffiare* to scratch). Among the foremost known practitioners of sgraffito were Isaac Stout of Bucks County, who was active towards the end of the 18th century, as was George Hubener in Montgomery County, and David Spinner, also of Bucks County, who specialised in hunting and equestrian scenes and who was active at the beginning of the 19th century. Peter Schmidt, a Swiss potter, was working in Ohio towards the end of the 18th century until about 1840, while Henry Roudebuth, Jacob Scholl and Samuel Troxel, all of Montgomery County, were working about 1830. Sgraffito plates and dishes, the main types of objects of this kind, were almost always made for weddings, anniversaries and similar celebrations.

Another important source of folk ceramics were certain German and Swiss religious communities. The most important of these was the Moravian settlement at Bethabara, North Carolina, where, by 1756, one of the most outstanding figures in the history of early American ceramics, Gottfried Aust, was working.

Born in Germany, Aust was already a skillful potter before moving to Bethabara, which was the first pottery in the state. In 1771, he moved on to another Moravian settlement at Salem, which had been established in 1768 and which lasted until 1830. Apart from learning to make stoneware here, he

was also shown the method of manufacturing Wedgwood's famous Queensware by an English potter called William Ellis, who had come to America with the unsuccessful John Bartlam in 1766. Brother Aust died in 1788.

Early Moravian pottery is of good quality and simple in form and glaze, the latter usually being plain black. Indeed, they mirror perfectly the austere surroundings in which they were made. The later Moravian settlement at Salem made fine stoneware, which was also the main product of the Harmony Society's pottery works at Economy, Pennsylvania. The latter's work tends to be more decorated, however, since the Harmonists, unlike the Moravians, traded with the outside world.

At Zoar, Ohio, a community of strictly enclosed German Pietists started a pottery in about 1817 under the leadership of Solomon Purdy, which made plain but beautiful redware vessels. Neither the Harmonists' nor the Moravians' ceramics are marked although a few Zoar pieces are marked ZOAR, with asterisks after the first three letters. It is also worth noting that a unique piece of pottery, the earthenware horn, was used at the Zoarite community of Tuscarawas County, Ohio, to call field workers in to meals and prayers.

While stylistically different from New England wares, Pennsylvania pieces also came in a wider range. Pie plates and dishes were frequently made in the latter state in addition to the flasks, bottles and storage jars which were about all the New England potters produced. However, by the end of the 18th century, the German settlers had spread throughout all the then civilised areas and towards the end of the earthenware period, the two styles began to merge, although New England potters always retained a distinctive restraint.

Stoneware, a harder and less porous type of ceramic than earthenware, was probably produced in America towards the end of the 17th century, although the first known dated piece was made by Joseph Thiekson of New Jersey in 1722. It was about this time also, that Anthony Duché, a Huguenot immigrant, is recorded as making stoneware in Philadelphia.

The leading centres of production at the beginning of the stoneware period were New York, New Jersey and Philadelphia. This was because large deposits of suitable, and easily transportable, clay were found in the vicinities. The most extensive deposits were found at Bayonne, New Jersey, on the northern shores of Staten Island and at Huntingdon, Long Island. New York also produced what was unquestionably the most important stoneware works of the 18th century, the Corselius, later Crolius, factory, founded by William Crolius, a native of Coblenz, Germany, who came to New York in 1718. From 1730, this factory continued to produce fine stoneware flagons, jars and bottles until it closed in 1887.

Crolius' brother-in-law, John Remmey, also from Germany, started another pottery directly adjacent to Crolius' and the two continued as rivals until they were merged in 1820. The Crolius factory produced an enormous amount in its 150 year life and some of its more common marks are as follows:

An amusing 19th-century slipware bird whistle, possibly from Pennsylvania.

Adam States founded a successful factory at Greenwich, Connecticut, in about 1750 and members of his family established other factories at New London, Stonington and Norwich. Between the 1730s and 1760s, William Rogers was producing extremely high quality pieces at Yorktown, Virginia, while another son of Anthony Duché of Philadelphia, Andrew, was active in South Carolina and Georgia in the 1730s.

Large deposits of clay were also found in Ohio in the second decade of the 19th century and continued to be found up until the 1840s; factories started up in many towns, including Zanesville, which, later in the century, was to become an important centre for art pottery.

In the mid 18th century, salt-glazing, a technique developed in Germany and the Lowlands in the 17th century, first began to be used and drove another nail in the coffin of the earthenware potter. For some time there had been doubts about the danger from poisoning from earthenware lead-glazes, and salt-glazes seemed to be the answer. The Germans of Pennsylvania continued to make earthenware until late in the 19th century but also produced fine stoneware and in larger quantities than earthenware.

The mid 19th century effectively saw the end of the folk pottery tradition with its small kilns and itinerant potters. The growth of commercialism, the great industrial expansion of mid-century America, placed a pressure of demand upon such potters that they could not survive. Earthenware and stoneware had not much changed in America since they had first been made. The *nouveau riche* of the large cities and the old-established merchant classes, however, did not consider folk pottery worthy of use in their homes; until higher class wares, especially tablewares which were seldom made by the folk potter, were produced in the United States, such people would continue to import what they needed from Europe and China, the latter country having built up a flourishing porcelain trade with America. American manufacturers, spurred on by the knowledge that there were domestic markets to be won, concentrated on producing sophisticated pottery and porcelain, and in producing it in large quantities. This was the end of the individual craftsman for some time.

Before going on to discuss the most important commercial potteries, however, it is time to look at the porcelain industry. The first porcelain made in England was produced at the Bow factory, thirty-six years after the technique of manufacturing hard-paste porcelain in the Chinese manner was discovered at Meissen in Germany in 1710. In America, no porcelain was produced before the 1820s although Andrew Duché, during his stay in Savannah, Georgia, discovered that the Cherokee Indian clay of that region was identical to the fine white kaolin needed for porcelain, and it was probably he who later supplied this clay to the Bow factory. There is also some evidence, although only slight, that he may have produced himself some proto-porcelain at this time (he claimed to have made two cups). But this is a mere historical curiosity.

The history of American porcelain before about 1825 is

1 I.C.
2 C. CROLIUS/MANHATTAN WELLS/NEW YORK
3 C. CROLIUS/MANUFACTURER/MANHATTAN WELLS/NEW YORK
4 C. CROLIUS NYC
5 C. CROLIUS/NEW YORK
6 C. CROLIUS/MANUFACTURER/NEW YORK

The first mark is that of John Crolius, about 1775. Marks 2 and 3 are those of Clarkson Crolius I, and were in use between 1795 and 1815. Mark 4 is also that of Clarkson Crolius I but was in use between 1800 and 1825. Mark 5 is that of Clarkson Crolius I and II, and was in use between 1815 and 1848, while mark 6 is that of Clarkson Crolius II and was in use between about 1825 and 1870.

Other important New York stoneware makers included Commeraw's Pottery of Corlears Hook, in existence between 1800 and 1820, N. Clark Jnr of Athens, which in about 1830 became the Clark & Fox Pottery Company, White's Pottery of Utica (about 1865–70), the Boone Pottery of Brooklyn, the William A. Macquoid Pottery Works at Little West 12th Street, New York City, which lasted from 1864 to 1870 and Israel Seymour of Troy, who was working at the beginning of the 19th century.

Stoneware was not produced in much quantity in New England and the first attempt by Isaac Parker in 1740, with the help of James Duché, son of Anthony, ended somewhat disastrously in 1745. The only really successful maker was William Seaver of Taunton, Massachusetts, who produced good quality pieces from about 1772 until 1790. The Dutchman

76 Early 19th-century Staffordshire spatterware plate made specifically for the provincial American market.

essentially a history of European and Chinese imports, with the latter, especially K'ang Hsi blue and white, predominant. By 1767, a New York merchant could advertise 'India China, enamelled and blue and white bowls caudle cups &c . . .' Blue and white from the Liverpool and Worcester factories was also imported in reasonably large quantities although the fact that Liverpool was one of the major ports for American trade and Worcester was close to another, Bristol, meant that ceramics could be exported at minimum cost. Leeds also exported many pieces as did Staffordshire, although the majority of the latter's wares was pottery.

Staffordshire was also famous for its spatterware, so-called because the plates and dishes etc. appeared to have been literally spattered with colour; this was made specifically for the American market around 1820–60 as was another type of Staffordshire pottery, the gaily coloured 'Gaudy Dutch Ware'.

Philadelphia, the great late 18th-century cultural centre of America, not surprisingly produced the first porcelain factory known to have been established in the new republic. Bonnin and Morris in 1770 made soft-paste porcelain of surprisingly high quality, of which about twenty pieces have survived. This shaky and short-lived venture had little effect upon the general situation however. Chinese and English porcelain continued to be imported while in the early 19th century, a feeling of kinship with another new republic, France, caused a considerable influx of French porcelain, which was especially patronised by American presidents. White House services from this period include examples from Sèvres, Nast, Dagoty, Rue D'Angoulême and Niderviller factories while the sixth President, John Quincy Adams, went one further and ordered a Berlin-Meissen service, although this showed the continued popularity of blue and white, being of the so-called Onion pattern.

French designs influenced the work of America's first successful manufacturer of porcelain, William Ellis Tucker, whose factory was established in Philadelphia in 1825 and which lasted until 1838, although after the latter date, Tucker ceased manufacturing porcelain and instead imported it from Europe. Tucker's elegant pieces, including his famous pitchers, were usually decorated with floral patterns and gilded. They were rarely marked although the moulder's incised initials appear on the base of a small number of pieces. The forms were derived from French Neo-classical porcelain and were of good, but not exceptional, quality. Before the factory ceased operation it was also known as Tucker & Hulme and Tucker & Hemphill.

In the 1840s, two important firms, the United States Pottery Company and the Union Porcelain Works, produced the unglazed biscuit-like porcelain called Parian, while they and other companies also produced that light opalescent porcelain called Belleek. The firm of Knowles, Taylor & Knowles named their variety Lotusware. At this point, however, we may merge back with commercial pottery since all the companies manufacturing at this time were also producing sophisticated stoneware.

77 Chinese export porcelain with Fitzhugh border and the arms of the United States.

78 Leeds dinner plate bearing the arms of the United States, about 1790–1820.

78

79 A Tuckerware porcelain pitcher, dated 1828. The American Museum in Britain, Bath.

80 A Rookwood Pottery vase, 1890, painted
by Matthew Daley. Typical 'Mahogany' glaze
and floral decoration, the most famous
Rookwood decorative scheme.

The Rookwood Pottery monograms
from 1886 to 1900.

The growth of the commercial pottery industry did not have its roots only in the mass production methods necessary to cope with the massive new demand for domestic products. Combined with this was a desire on the part of the American potteries to compete on level terms aesthetically with the ceramics of Europe and the East. Harold F. Guilland, in his book *American Folk Pottery* states the situation clearly:

'The great fairs such as the New York Exposition of 1853 and the Centennial Exposition of 1876 at Philadelphia were also factors which led to the breakdown in the traditional crafts. The fairs emphasised the technological advances and their advantages in the factory, on the farm, and in the home. At the Centennial Exhibition in 1876 a large collection of classical forms and Oriental art were shown for the first time. Many potters were greatly inspired and a trend towards art wares and knick-knacks began to develop. Potters who had the benefit of some artistic training began to develop a greater variety of glazes, and to consciously create objects of art patterned after the ancient wares of China and Greece. Until this time, beauty in American pottery had been a spontaneous, subconscious expression in wares primarily for utilitarian purposes.'

The way had already been shown, however, by firms which began in the second and third decades of the 19th century. Thus in the 1820s, Thomas Haig & Company of Philadelphia were producing sophisticated glazed red earthenware far removed from the folk pottery tradition, while D. & J. Henderson's American Pottery Company of Jersey City, New Jersey, was active between 1828 and 1845 producing fine transfer-printed wares very similar to those from Staffordshire. Two important factories were founded at Greenpoint, Long Island, towards the end of the 1840s, Charles Cartlidge & Company, which existed from 1848 to 1856 and William Boch & Brother, founded in 1850, taken over by Thomas C. Smith in 1862 and renamed the Union Porcelain Works; this factory finally closed in 1910. Smith employed the designer Karl Mueller, whose extravagant exhibition pieces of porcelain rivalled Tiffany & Company for their exuberant vulgarity. Early Boch pieces, made before the factory was taken over by Smith, and marked WB&BR'S/GREENPOINTL.I., are very rare and sought-after collectors' items. Another factory, started in 1853, and lasting until 1888, was James Cair's New York Pottery, which specialised in tablewares and Parian figures.

Of all the commercial potteries, the best known and most important is the factory at Bennington, Vermont. It was started by John Norton in 1795 and produced earthenware although by 1815, stoneware was almost the exclusive product. In 1837, one of the most significant figures in the history of American ceramics, Christopher Webber Fenton, joined the firm and in 1843, Julius Norton, grandson of John, and Fenton entered into a partnership and brought over John Harrison from the Copeland factory in England to manage the newly organised firm. In 1853, the factory was named the United States Pottery Company.

Fenton's main claim to fame was his use of the 'flint enamel glaze', a process which he patented in 1849, by which time it had probably been in use at Bennington for nearly a decade. This glaze is a variation on the mottled brown glaze found on pieces made at the Rockingham factory in England, which was first produced in the 18th century; for this reason, Bennington and Rockingham are interchangeable names in America for things so decorated, although Rockingham, strictly speaking, should only be applied to English pieces.

Although the brown mottled type of Rockingham glaze was certainly in use in American factories before its introduction at Bennington, Fenton's contribution was to develop a method whereby the glaze became far more colourful, incorporating greens, blues, yellows and orange. Animals thus glazed are perhaps the most famous products of the Bennington factory – lions, deer, poodles etc. – and they also made slightly whimsical bottles and flasks. Later in its career, the United States 81 Pottery Company produced a type of Belleek ware which, in allusion to the white Chinese porcelain, they called *Blanc-de-chine*.

Towards the end of the 19th century, as a direct result of the Arts and Crafts movement's bitter, if losing, campaign against mass production, small individual potteries employing artists and designers dedicated to the idea of the perfect, hand-made piece, sprang up all over Europe, and the movement quickly spread to America.

Although the period around 1880 is generally accepted as the beginning of art pottery in America, one firm, the Robertsons' Chelsea Keramic Art Works of Chelsea, Massachusetts, was founded in 1866 and was perhaps the 'father' of the movement. The earliest pieces of Chelsea pottery were, in fact, straight copies of Greek *krater* and urns but in the 1880s, they began experimenting with Oriental glazes, producing beautiful *sang de boeuf* pieces in the 1880s and fine 'Japanese crackleware' glazes in the 1890s. In 1895, the factory moved to Dedham, Massachusetts and was renamed the Dedham Pottery Works; the main product of the reorganised factory was a very popular blue and white tableware.

The greatest American art pottery, and one of the most important anywhere in the world, was the Rookwood Pottery, 8▌ founded by Maria Longworth Nichols in 1880 in Cincinnati. In fact some six factories were founded in this city between 1879 and 1880 but Rookwood was the only one to achieve lasting success; the other five were the T. J. Wheatley Pottery, the Avon Pottery, the M. Louise McLaughlin factory, which produced wares called Losanti, the Matt Morgan Art Pottery, and the Cincinnati Art Pottery.

Mrs Nichols, one of the most remarkable women in the history of the applied arts, brought over an experienced art potter from England, Joseph Bailey, and also, two years later, employed William Watts Taylor as general manager.

The earliest pieces were carved, incised, stamped or impressed, were applied in high relief, were often gilt and employed either overglaze or underglaze slip; in other words, the pottery was feeling its way and experimenting with a variety of different techniques. Two underglaze slip colour

schemes – one with a pinkish-white ground called 'Cameo' and the other with a brown-orange-yellow glaze called 'Mahogany' – proved the most popular and were soon known under the collective name of Standard Rookwood.

From the mid 1880s onwards, the factory experimented further and produced a number of specifically named types: the gold-speckled adventurine glaze marketed in 1884 under the name 'Tiger eye' (this was an accidental process and examples are extremely rare and highly prized), various background-colour pieces called 'Iris', 'Sea green' and 'Aerial blue', all first produced in 1890; the matt glazes introduced by Artus van Briggle in 1896 and widely used by Rookwood from 1901 onwards; and from 1904, a transparent matt glaze called 'Vellum'. From 1890 onwards, the floral decoration most commonly associated with Rookwood was widely used, as well as animals and portraits of Indians. A few pieces had silver overlays by the Gorham Company.

In 1889, William Watts Taylor became sole owner of the Rookwood factory and the company's international success was assured in 1900, when it won a Gold Medal at the great *Exposition Universelle* in Paris. In 1913, Taylor died and although the factory continued until 1941, it ceased to produce pieces of much aesthetic interest after its owner's death.

One of the greatest attractions of Rookwood for the collector, apart from its self-evident quality, is the fact that each piece is unique and has no duplicate. Added recommendations are that each piece is signed and dated by the artist responsible. From 1880 to 1881, each piece bears the words ROOK-WOOD POTTERY and the date. From 1882–1886, this changed to the single word ROOKWOOD and the date; from 1886, the monogram RP was used as the Rookwood mark, although it had been used by the decorator Brennan from 1883. From 1887, the date was marked by a flame point above the monogram – one point being added every year until 1900. In 1901, the monogram, surrounded by fourteen flames, became the standard mark, the years of the new century being shown by Roman numerals.

As we have said, each piece was individually signed by the artist responsible for the decoration. The most important painters were probably Albert R. Valentien, who was the chief decorator from 1881 to 1905, Artus van Briggle, K. Shirayamadani, W. P. McDonald, Clara Chipman Newton, Laura Fry and Maria Longworth Nichols, the founder of the factory.

Rookwood spread its influence throughout America. Artus van Briggle left the factory in 1901 and opened his van Briggle Pottery at Colorado Springs. He produced interesting pieces in swirled Art Nouveau shapes and decorated with the matt glazes he had been responsible for introducing to Rookwood. Van Briggle died in 1904 and although the factory was carried on by his wife, the quality declined sharply.

Laura Fry, who is also listed above as a Rookwood decorator, helped William A. Long found the Lonhuda Factory at Steubenville, Ohio, in 1892. In 1895, this was merged with Samuel A. Weller's commercial pottery factory at Zanesville, Ohio and renamed Lowelsa, with variations of the pieces produced being known as Aurelian and Eocean. Their pieces, strongly reminiscent of Rookwood wares, were similarly decorated with flowers, animals and American Indians. They also produced a rather garish pottery called Dickensware, with characters from Dickens' novels illustrating each piece but compensated for this by producing an extremely beautiful irridescent lustreware called Sicardo after its designer, the Frenchman Jacques Sicard. These wonderful pieces have a somewhat similar appearance to Tiffany's Favrile glass; a variety of Sicardo with landscape scenes was called Lasa.

Long himself did not stay with the newly merged company, moving in 1886 to the J. B. Owens Pottery Company at Zanesville. He did, however, take his approach to design with him and the Owen products, called Utopian, are very similar to Lowelsa, and hence to Rookwood, pieces. Ceramics made by this company are of reasonable quality and were produced until 1907, when the factory closed.

A late Zanesville pottery was the Roseville Art Pottery, which was founded in Roseville, Ohio, in 1892 and moved to Zanesville nine years later. Again, pieces produced here are very similar to Rookwood and only pieces bearing the words ROZANE or ROZANE ROYALE are of any interest to collectors, since the later wares bearing the impressed mark ROSEVILLE are extremely common and of indifferent quality.

Two factories need to be mentioned finally. In 1897, Mary Shearer of the Cincinnati Art Academy, who was well-acquainted with Rookwood pottery, moved to New Orleans to organise the Newcombe Pottery, which was part of the Sophie Newcombe Memorial College for Women. Not surprisingly, this factory concentrated initially on producing Rookwood-like pieces but these were of poor quality compared to the original. Newcombe later developed its own distinctively shaped pieces with fine dark glazes, which changed to matt after 1910. In East Boston, Massachusetts, William H. Gruely's Gruely Faience & Tile Company produced art pottery until 1910; their swirled, Art Nouveau, monochrome pieces are somewhat similar to the products of the van Briggle Pottery.

FIREARMS

72

82 Presentation 1851 Navy Colt revolver in its case. This example is inscribed 'Admiral Sir Thomas Cochran from the Inventor'. W. Keith Neal Collection, England.

The history of American firearms before the third quarter of the 19th century is essentially the history of European, and especially English, guns. The great exceptions are the Kentucky rifles, also called Lancaster Valley or Pennsylvania rifles; these were made by the German settlers in Pennsylvania during the 18th century. Like the other crafts associated with the Pennsylvania 'Dutch', their guns were adaptations of the pieces they had known at home and had brought with them. The Kentucky is an evolution of the German Jaeger, or hunting rifle, and has a barrel length of between forty and forty-five inches. This barrel is usually octagonal, with the maker's name marked on the top face.

In common with most 18th-century long guns, the barrel was attached to the stock by pins passing through the wood and engaged with lugs fitted beneath the barrel. The stocks themselves were most commonly of 'curly' maple or walnut, and were occasionally figured to give a false, but decorative, grain. A few examples have carved stocks but the majority are fitted with inlaid brass, which usually included a cover for a patch box fitted into the butt.

An important reason for the gun's efficiency was the loading of the bullets wrapped in greased linen patches, which not only increased the rate of fire but also ensured that the grooves of the rifling were kept fairly clean, as the linen was dispatched through the barrel on firing.

During the 18th century, the majority of flintlock firearms were imported from England. Nevertheless, a few enterprising American craftsmen produced interesting variations, one of whom, Captain Artemas Wheeler of Concord, Massachusetts, patented 'a mechanism for a seven-shot gun'. Although details of this have been lost, it was almost certainly similar to the revolver patented in London in 1818 by an extremely important American gunsmith, Elisha Haydon Collier of Boston, who carried on his business in England, after having been an associate of Wheeler in the United States. The importance of Collier's patent was that it was the first to ensure that a revolver could be fired without risk of explosion. Hitherto, gas had escaped into the second chamber after the first firing; Collier's revolvers had a gas-tight joint between the chamber and the barrel, brought about by a steel wedge being pushed forward at the moment of firing, from behind the falling cock.

Initially, Collier's guns had automatically rotating cylinders, but this system was abandoned for a hand-operated one; only one revolver of the former type is now known, and even this has been converted to a hand-rotated system. Like so many of the great craftsmen we have met in these pages, Collier was a designer years ahead of his time, and met the usual fate of such men, achieving no financial success.

In 1836, Benjamin and Barton Darling, two minor American gunsmiths, patented a single-action pepperbox gun. From the 17th century onwards, gunsmiths had been attempting to produce an efficient multi-shot gun, and there were two obvious alternatives – either revolving chambers or revolving barrels. The former type proved the most efficient but for several years, multi-barreled pepperbox or pepperpot pistols

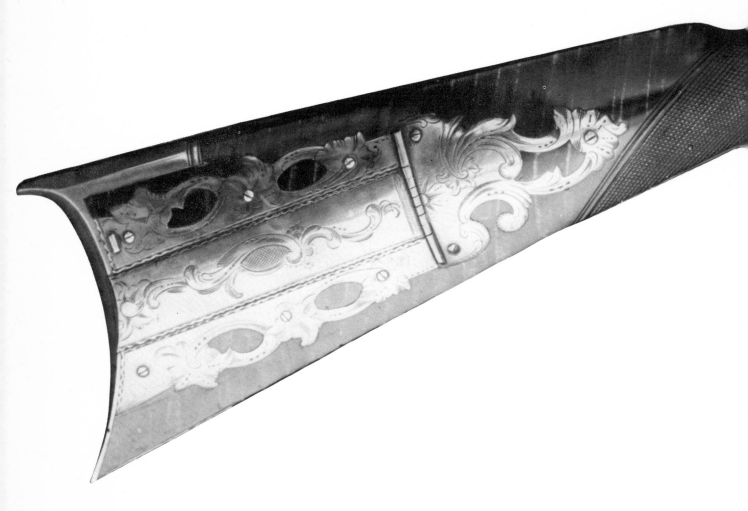

were produced. On the Darlings' gun, the barrels rotated when the piece was cocked but in 1837, Ethan Allen was granted a patent for a self-cocking pepperpot on which the barrel rotated and the gun was fired by one pressure on the trigger. Pepperpots were heavy and unwieldy pieces and their popularity was short-lived.

We should perhaps mention two curious types of guns, one of which, the bowie-knife-pistol, was patented by George Elgin of Georgia in 1837. In fact, there was nothing in the least original about Elgin's combination firearm and edged weapon, such pieces having been made in Europe from the 16th century onwards. Elgin's example consisted of a single-shot percussion pistol, the barrel running part of the way along the blunt edge of a massive bowie knife. This cumbersome object can hardly be described as a functional weapon, any more than the ingenious six-barrel pepperbox pistol with the barrels rotating around the tang of a two-edged sword, which was patented by Robert L. Lawton of Newport, Rhode Island, in the same year.

Surprisingly enough, however, Elgin's bowie-knife-guns did enjoy a short-lived success, being produced in large numbers by two companies, C. B. Allen of Springfield, Massachusetts (the blades being made by the Ames Manufacturing Company) and by Morrill, Mosman & Blair of Amerst, who made both the guns and the blades.

In contrast to these rather ungainly firearms, one of the most famous types of American gun, the deringer, is a large-bored but small-framed pocket pistol, invented by Henry Deringer of Philadelphia (1786–1868), and first manufactured by him in the late 1820s. It was widely used and gained some measure of international notoriety through being used by John Wilkes Booth to assassinate Abraham Lincoln.

The deringer was also widely copied and cunning manufacturers frequently used Deringer's name misspelt 'Derringer' to describe their pieces and by so doing, avoided infringing the original inventor's patent; in some cases, however, they did not bother to change the spelling, and many pistols are known signed 'Deringer' but not by Henry Deringer himself. To the

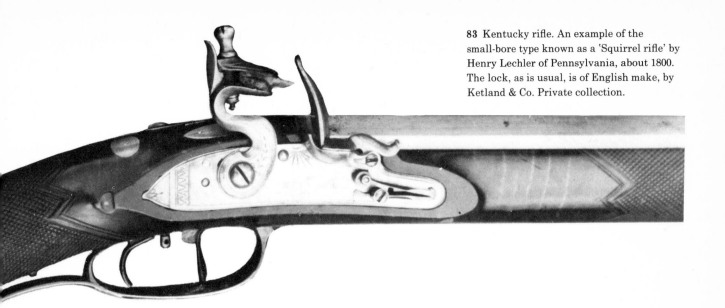

gun collector today, 'deringer' describes the inventor's own examples, which are now very rare, while 'derringer' is used as a generic name for pocket pistols in his style.

Samuel Colt is certainly the greatest gunsmith of the 19th century and one of the most important figures in the whole history of the craft. He brought to a head a century of experimentation and may be called the father of the modern firearm. Born in Hartford, Connecticut in 1814, Colt's first revolver was devised in the 1830s, when he was in his early twenties. This was a muzzle-loading, percussion-cap revolver with an automatically rotating cylinder; this cylinder was made to revolve by means of a ratchet-and-pawl system which may have been inspired by the device used to drive the wheels of a paddle-steamer. This mechanism was not, in fact, entirely original, a similar system having been devised by an otherwise unknown 17th-century English gunsmith called John Dafte of London.

The initial experiments with Colt's revolver were carried out by two American gunsmiths, Anton Chase and John Pearson, with finance provided by a lecture tour given by Colt, in which he demonstrated the effects of laughing gas! The revolver was patented in America and England in 1836 and in the same year, production began at the Patent Arms Manufacturing Company's factory at Paterson, New Jersey (hence the name Colt Paterson given to these early pieces).

Yet again, however, the work of a great innovator was not appreciated and the company went into liquidation in 1841. It was only the outbreak of the American-Mexican War six years later which gave Colt his chance. The American Government ordered one thousand Colt revolvers, which were made under licence by Eli Whitney at his factory at Whitneyville, Connecticut, production starting in 1847. This was an improved version of the Colt Paterson, and is variously called the Walker, Whitneyville-Walker, or Model 1847 Colt. The name Walker refers to Captain Samuel S. Walker of the Texas Militia, who suggested some of the modifications. This gun, weighing four pounds, nine ounces, is a .44 calibre six-shot single-action percussion revolver with a nine-inch barrel. It represented an advance on the five-shot .28 calibre Colt Paterson.

The money accruing from this Government contract

enabled Colt to start his own factory on Pearl Street, Hartford, Connecticut. This was in production for seven years, moving in 1855 to a site on the Connecticut river. Between 1848 and his death in 1862, Colt produced several different types of revolver, all of which are now keenly collected.

In 1848, he marketed a six-shot Dragoon revolver, also known as the 'Old Model Army Revolver'; this was of .44 calibre and had a barrel length of 7½ inches. The same year saw the introduction of a five-shot, rammer-less, pocket revolver of .31 calibre with a choice of barrel lengths ranging between three and six inches. A similar pocket revolver, but with a rammer, was produced in 1849, while in 1851, another Navy Colt, and a lighter version of the same, were marketed.

In 1857, the first solid frame Colt revolver was produced. Previously, revolvers were made up of barrel-frame assemblies held together by a transverse pin. The new Colt, designed by Elisha K. Root, the factory superintendent, but later the president of the company, was a considerable improvement on any previous revolver. The most famous of all Colt hand-guns, the 'Peacemaker' or 'Frontier six-shooter', was not developed until 1873, eleven years after Colt's death. This was a solid frame single-action gate-loaded gun with a choice of calibres ranging from .22 to .476, and five different barrel lengths. Five years later, another famous Colt, the double-action, solid-framed, gate-loading piece known as the 'Lightning' was marketed.

Finally we should mention Smith and Wesson's Winchester repeating rifle, almost as famous in the folklore of the 'Old West' as the Colt Peacemaker; by a coincidence, both guns were first introduced in the same year, 1863. The Winchester, a lever-action, under-barrel magazine repeater, was in fact a development of an earlier type of American rifle, the Jennings.

Walter Hall and Lewis Jennings had, through their agent Stephen Taylor, patented in London a bullet containing its own propellant charge, together with a lever-action repeating rifle. The American patents, the cartridge to Hall and the rifle to Jennings, were granted in 1849. The major breakthrough represented by this rifle was the cartridge which, because of its self-contained propellant, obviated the fouling of the barrel by loose black powder which had previously held back the development of an efficient repeating rifle.

84 Bird decoys. *left to right* Canvas back drake made in about 1900 in the St Lawrence river area, New York State; golden plover, about 1900; pintail made by H. Keyes Chadwick of Martha's Vineyard, Massachusetts, about 1910; hen broadbill by Ben Schmidt, about 1890. James Dugdale Collection, London.

85 Cigar-store Indian known as Seneca John. Collections of Greenfield Village and the Henry Ford Museum, Dearborn, Michigan.

86 *The Roseate Spoonbill,* one of the most colourful plates from John James Laforest Audubon's *The Birds of America.*

Toys and Dolls

Although a number of dolls and games from the 18th century and earlier have survived, the majority of antique American toys date from roughly 1830–1900. Toys from this latter period, in spite of the fact that many were produced by highly organised commercial enterprises, nevertheless retain that naivety and freshness of vision so characteristic of folk art. Like the duck decoys made by industrial methods, 19th-century toys and dolls constitute one of the few areas of the applied arts where the individually made pieces vary little in quality from factory produced examples.

One of the earliest and most important American toymakers was William S. Tower of South Hingham, Massachusetts, who in the 1830s, founded the Tower Toy Company. Making extremely decorative wooden toys and dolls' houses, one of Tower's associates, Loring Cushing, who joined the firm in 1861, specialised in wooden miniature furniture for dolls' houses, pieces which are now amongst the most sought-after of all American toys.

Although wood was the most frequently used material, tin and cast iron were also employed in toymaking, the most important manufacturers being the Philadelphia Tin Toy Manufactory, George W. Brown and J. & E. Stearns. Of the last two named, Brown specialised in tin and Stearns in iron; they amalgamated in the early 1860s to form the American Toy Company. Amongst their most famous products were the distinctively American form of banks or money boxes – 'Uncle Sam', 'Tammany Hall', 'Monkeys up a tree' and 'Frogs'.

Nevertheless, wood continued to be used by the majority of toymakers, the greatest of whom were Jesse A. Crandall and Charles A. Crandall. The Crandall family was to toys what the Townsend-Goddard family was to furniture; eleven Crandalls were toymakers and their activities span the 19th century. Jesse and Charles were cousins who, as far as is known, had no personal contact; their most famous toys, however, are very similar. Jesse patented the ever-popular hollow pentagonal nesting blocks painted with numbers and letters, whilst Charles invented building blocks, still found in every house throughout the world where there are children. Charles also invented, in 1889, the so-called 'Pigs-in-clover' maze game, in which four balls or 'pigs' have to be run into the central compartment of the maze simultaneously. This game, and pocket plastic versions of it, is still sold in most toy shops.

In the late 1860s and 1870s, clockwork and other mechanical toys were introduced by such companies at Althof, Bergman & Company and E.R. Ives, the latter being one of the first to produce a model railway engine complete with track. Ives also produced some particularly popular clockwork figure toys, such as bicycle riders etc., while probably the most famous American mechanised doll was Enoch Morrison's 'Autoperipatetikos' patented in 1862 which, as its Greek name implies, walked automatically. Vocal dolls were also popular and included Edison's 'Phonographic Doll' of 1878 and William Webber's 'Singing Doll' of 1882.

87 Wooden toys, an oxcart and farmers carved by a Vermont farmer and his son, about 1860. The Essex Institute, Salem, Massachusetts.

Although all the toys we have discussed have been 19th century, the most well-known American doll is in fact 20th century, the world famous 'Kewpie Doll' designed by Ernesto Peruggi in about 1920 and produced by the Manhattan Toy & Doll Manufacturing Company. In the popular imagination, 'Kewpies' are as American as Coca-Cola or hamburgers.

Needlework

Two types of needlework were produced in some quantity in America – samplers and patchwork quilts.

The sampler, the name being an abbreviated form of the word 'exemplar', served a dual purpose. It was primarily an anthology of stitches, which the housewife could always refer to. Secondly, because if you were going to have a repertoire of stitches, you might as well depict something useful, it was embroidered with an alphabet, which would serve to teach the children of the family to read and write. In Europe in the 16th and 17th centuries, the first use was the main one but during the 18th century, the presence of the alphabet became of prime importance.

Stemming from the alphabet came a third function; if you were going to stitch letters, you might as well have them say something instructive. Thus, whilst many samplers are embroidered with religious texts, by far the most interesting from an historic viewpoint are the geneological ones, some of which give the details of births, marriages and deaths of several generations of one family. Thus the famous Ohmstead sampler, made in Connecticut in 1774, lists twelve members of the family, giving their dates of birth and marriage.

The majority of American samplers date from the 18th and early 19th centuries, but since the practice of making them goes back to the 15th century in Europe, it seems probable that they were made in some quantity by the early settlers, especially as their practical value would be greater than it was in Europe. Only two American 17th-century samplers survive, however, the Loara Standish sampler of about 1640, preserved at Pilgrim Hall, Plymouth, Massachusetts, and Ann Gover's sampler now owned by the Essex Institute, Salem, Massachusetts.

As the practical importance of samplers waned towards the end of the 18th century, they became increasingly more decorative, developing into embroidered pictorial compositions of great charm, depicting houses, gardens, hunting scenes etc.

Patchwork quilts are also popular with collectors. It is probable that most of them were brides' quilts since it was customary for women to make, at sewing bees, a dozen quilts as part of a girl's trousseau. The best quilt was often made out of two or three materials specially bought for the purpose, while the others were made from odd scraps of material, sewn together either in geometric patterns or in irregular shapes – these latter are known as crazy quilts. Most quilts date from the 19th century, although some of the materials used may be older.

Metalwork

Pewter has always been considered the poor man's silver and this was unquestionably its reason for existence – to replace the fine silverware of the aristocracy and the rich merchant classes. Pewter is an alloy of tin, which is the predominant metal, copper, antimony, bismuth and lead. In old pewter, silver was never added purposely, although small quantities are found since tin in its rough state usually contains small quantities of the precious metal. During the Art Nouveau period, however, some makers did include quite a significant amount of silver in order to give the metal a richer appearance. Also, in the finest old pewter, there is no lead.

Pewter was worked in medieval times in Europe and it is known that the first settlers in America brought plates, dishes and beakers with them. Thus in 1635, Sarah Dillingham, a widow, died at Ipswich, Connecticut, leaving 40½ pounds of pewter which was valued at £2.14.0. As with silver, pewter suffered damage and it is likely that the first American pewterers were not in fact makers but repairers and importers. In the 17th and early 18th centuries, some ten pewterers are recorded as having been working in Salem, Boston, New York and Philadelphia.

American pewter made before 1750 is of exceptional rarity and hardly any pieces are known; indeed, fully authenticated examples dating from between 1765 and 1775 are also extremely scarce. Known pewterers working in the second half of the 18th century include Francis and Frederick Bassett of New York, Peter Young of Albany, New York, William and Cor-

nelius Bradford of New York and Philadelphia, Henry Will of New York and William Will of Philadelphia, Michael Lee of Taunton, Massachusetts, Gershom Jones of Providence, Rhode Island and Thomas and Joseph Danforth of Norwich, Connecticut and Jamestown, Massachusetts.

The effective history of American pewter spans a period between 1750 and 1850, during which time just over two hundred pewterers are recorded. Of the names listed above, Francis Bassett is probably the most highly regarded. Both he and Henry Will are known to have been working in New York by 1786 and are listed in the New York City Directory for that year, the two men being the earliest recorded makers in that city. Another Bassett, Frederick, was also working in New York at about the same time.

We have said that 18th-century American pewter is of extreme rarity and this fact is demonstrated by the extraordinary demand for it amongst collectors. In November 1971, an important and very rare pair of pewter chalices by Peter Young, Albany, New York, made in about 1784, with the cryptic engraving 'RBDC/Boght/1784', was sold at Sotheby Parke-Bernet for $5,250, the highest auction price achieved by any pewter of any age or country.

Pewter generally bears its maker's mark or 'touch' and in addition, much early English and American pewter bears a row of four small marks similar to the English silver hallmarks, which may not have been intended to mislead the purchaser into believing that he was actually buying a piece of silver, but certainly had that effect. Although in 1635, the Goldsmiths' Company succeeded in having a law passed forbidding pewter to be marked thus, no one appears to have taken much notice and such marks continued to be used until the 19th century.

In addition, there was a rose and crown mark which, under the rules of the English Society of Pewterers, could only be used by English pewterers on pieces made for sale outside London, and could not be accompanied by any other mark, device or touch. These rules, especially the latter one, were ignored, of course, by American pewterers (as they were by some English makers). A further mark was an 'x' which, in England, was supposed to denote a metal of very high quality. This too, was a mark used, or rather abused, by both English and American pewterers.

For the non-specialist, it is particularly difficult to decide whether a piece of pewter is English or American. The few surviving examples of 18th-century American pewter do not present much of a problem, since they are generally marked, but 19th-century American pieces are very often not marked. In general, English pewter is hammer-finished, whilst American is not, but the issue is not clear-cut since Continental pewter is often non-hammer finished.

The styles of pewter in America changed very little between about 1750 and 1820, and the marks, generally speaking, follow the English custom, although from the immediate post-Revolutionary period onwards, the Federal eagle was used with increasing frequency. Nevertheless, the majority of

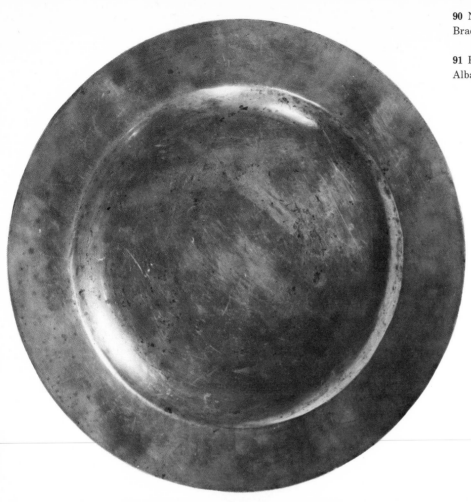

90 Nine inch pewter plate by Cornelius
Bradford, Philadelphia, about 1750–70.

91 Pair of pewter chalices by Peter Young,
Albany, New York, about 1784.

American pewter pieces between 1820 and 1830 are unmarked, although their similarity to Federal silver styles is a useful guide. In the end, however, this field, like that of early glass, requires above all, the instinct and acumen which only come with experience.

Another popular type of metalwork is painted tinware, sometimes called tôle, after the painted sheet iron popular in France during the Empire period and called *tôle peintre*. In pre-Revolutionary America, tin-plated sheet iron was imported from England and was extremely expensive and sparingly used. In the 19th century, however, the American tinware market flourished, and once again, the outstanding examples, superbly painted with gaily coloured fruit and flowers, were produced by the German settlers in Pennsylvania. The finest pieces were produced in the mid century and are now highly prized by collectors.

Folk art

The traditions of folk art in America, both fine and applied, is a particularly strong one. In Europe, only France can claim to have produced 'naive' painting on a level with American art of this type and the French reputation is largely based upon the work of three artists, Bauchant, Seraphine and, above all, Henri Rousseau. In the United States, folk art was raised to a high level of aesthetic achievement simply because many of its craftsmen and painters had little or no contact with 'sophisticated' culture and were merely producing something which they looked upon as functional.

This, of course, is the key. Much American applied art – bird decoys, ceramics, samplers, South Jersey glass – was primarily made to serve a purpose; in creating it, the craftsman had this object uppermost in his mind. The decorative element simply came from his 'naive' desire to make whatever it was 'pleasing'. The Shakers believed that the pleasure to be derived from an artifact stemmed from its ability to be completely useful. In a sense, their furniture is folk art, since it is totally outside the stylistic mainstream, was made with purely practical considerations in mind, with no compromise with fashion, and was made by self-taught workmen who did not have the pretensions of the successful city cabinetmaker. Indeed, I believe Shaker furniture to be folk art in its purest form, the highest and most enduring achievement of the tradition.

Fraktur is a folk art peculiar to Pennsylvania German settlers. A fraktur is usually a birth, baptismal or marriage certificate which, through an ornate and elaborate calligraphy, becomes a decorative picture. They are, therefore, quintessential types of folk art, in which itinerant scribes attempted to make mundane legal documents into attractive pictorial compositions which could then be proudly displayed. Good examples were produced well into the 19th century, and are embellished with watercolour drawings.

In about 1860, printed fraktur outlines were published, which were then hand-coloured; these are not, of course, nearly as interesting as the earlier hand-drawn and written examples. The word 'fraktur' is a contraction of *fraktur-schrift*, a word derived from a 16th-century German typeface.

Theorem paintings are coloured stencil compositions which were primarily intended for use on furniture, but which were frequently stencilled onto velvet panels, thus becoming an early form of 'painting by numbers'! The finest examples, produced in the early 19th century, are still-lifes, but there are also extremely attractive landscape compositions.

Apart from the carving of stems and sterns of ships, the profession of the sea produced an important type of marine art, scrimshaw, or, to use an old-fashioned word, scrimshander. These words should by right be applied to any object of bone carved by sailors but are now generally taken to refer to carved sperm whales' teeth. These are engraved, the lines of the engraving being filled in with ink and pigment, with a variety of nautical scenes, some of the finest being episodes from whaling. Most of the examples known today date from 19th century.

The making of ships' figureheads was an important source of employment for the 18th- and early 19th-century itinerant woodcarver, and the fact that some of them became extremely well-known is demonstrated by the fact that in 1828, John Rogers, president of the Naval Board, was appealed to by the officers of *USS Concord*, who felt that he could use his influence to persuade Laben S. Beecher of Boston, the most celebrated ships' carver of his day, to decorate their vessel. Beecher started as an apprentice carver in 1822, and his last commission was the decoration of *USS Constitution* in 1834. His place as the leading marine carver was taken by John Mason.

Other carvers included Samuel Anderson Robb, who is also well known for his circus carousel animals, having been apprenticed to the Sebastian Wagon Company who specialised in pieces of this kind. Robb was also, as we shall see, the greatest maker of cigar-store Indians. Towards the end of the century, the immense popularity of circuses and fairs provided employment for carvers who would, earlier in the century, have been engaged in carving ships' figureheads. The finest carousel horses were produced by Gustav Augustus Dentzel's Carousel Factory in Germanstown, Pennsylvania in the 1890s. America's greatest 18th-century academic sculptor, William Rush, famous for his masterpiece *The Spirit of Schuykill*, also started his career carving figureheads and cigar-store Indians.

Brathwait's *Smoking Age*, published in London in 1617, illustrates a tobacconist's sign in which the popular misconception of what an American Indian looked like, that is, a negro wearing a kilt, is shown smoking a pipe. Thus the Indian as an advertisement for tobacco has a history going back almost as far as the European discovery of the plant itself. In America, it was probably in use during the 18th century, but the earliest surviving examples, dating from the 1820s, are not the statuesque figures so well-known today, but flat boards, either painted or carved on both sides.

The prototype cigar-store Indian as it is known today was the work of John L. Cromwell, a Massachusetts ships' figure-head carver born in 1805. He opened his carving shop in 1831 at 179 Cherry Street, Lower Manhattan. The popular idea of 85 a cigar-store Indian, a Mohawk warrior brandishing a tomohawk in his right hand and holding a toga-like bearskin in his left, is the style associated with Cromwell.

In the 1840s, Cromwell took Thomas V. Brooks as an apprentice and in 1847 the latter, at the age of nineteen, opened his own shop at 260 South Street. During the 1850s, Brooks became the foremost manufacturer of cigar-store Indians, producing, it has been estimated, over two hundred figures a year. Amongst his workmen were Thomas Millard Jnr, who had previously acted as an assistant to William Rush, and Samuel Anderson Robb, the marine carver, who came to work for Brooks in the 1860s.

Robb's superb figures are generally considered the greatest of their kind. In 1876, he went into partnership with William Demuth who, in 1869, had started manufacturing cigar-store Indians in cast zinc. The variety of Robb's activities, which also illustrates the wide range of skills appertaining to most woodcarvers of the period, may be gained from one of his advertisements, which states that he was capable of making 'Show Figures and Carved Lettered Signs–TOBACCONIST SIGNS in a great variety, on hand and made to any design. Ship and Steamboat carving, Eagles, Heads, Block letters, Shoe, Dentist and Druggist Signs, etc.'

Bird decoys obviously had a completely functional purpose and if they are elegant and superbly coloured works of art, it is only because the various forms of wildfowl they were simulating were elegant and superbly coloured themselves. In charting the underlying functionalism of much folk art, we note with interest how similar this statement is to the quoted remarks made by the Shakers about their furniture.

84 The object of a decoy was to lure live birds of the same species to within range of the hunter's gun; thus to be effective, they had to be as accurate as possible. Yet the depiction of a natural object is subject to the idiosyncrasies of an individual artist's 'interpretation' of what a given thing looks like. If beauty is in the eye of the beholder, so indeed is appearance of any kind. It is this difference in interpretation which enables the experts to differentiate between individual makers and regions.

The majority of decoys date from between roughly 1850 and 1925, although the quantity and quality of pieces declines after 1918 when Congress brought the mass extermination of wild bird life under control by passing the Migratory Bird Treaty Act–although not before some species, the Labrador duck, passenger pigeon and heath hen, for instance, had been hunted to extinction.

There were three basic types of bird decoy: the floating variety, usually duck, geese and Brandt; 'stick-ups', which, as their name implies, were stuck into the ground by means of a short pole, and were usually shore birds such as sand-

tten, als Christian Braun und seiner ehlichen

ria ist ein Sohn zur Welt gebohren, als:

eformierten Eltern ist zur Welt gebohren im Jahr

1781 den 10 ten Tag November um 12 uhr

m Zeichen de

a den Enadenbund Gottes einverleibet, und von

rter Prediger und Diener des Worts Got=

getauft und genennet worden, wie

zeu:gen ware. Wilhelm Henrich Lawald und seine Frau

Oben gemeldete ist gebohren in America, im Staat

Northamton Caunty in Bethlehen Taunschip

1786.

a: Ist vom ersten Lebenstritt bis ins kühle Crab der Erden, Nur ein kurt gemessener
blick! Gehet unsre Kraft zurück, Und wir sind mit jedem Jahre, allzu reiff zur Todten=
Stunde, uns die leste Stimme weckt: Dan GOtt hat's mit seinem Munde, Keinem
er sein Haus nun wohl bestellt geht mit Freuden aus der Welt. Da die
Sicherheit hingegen; Ewigs Sterben kan erregen.

Henrich Otto.

94 Two walrus tusk scrimshaws, the one on the left decorated with the figure of Christopher Columbus and the Federal eagle.

pipers, curlews, plovers, snipe etc.; and cut-out silouettes called 'flatties', the finest examples of which are from the Cape Cod area. An unusual flatty is the owl, which was used to lure crows who, for some reason, congregate around and abuse single owls. Rare old flatties sometimes consist of two flat depictions of the bird hinged together at right angles which, from a distance, give a more three-dimensional impression.

Apart from several well-known individual craftsmen, the second half of the 19th century also saw the introduction of factory-made decoys, which were, at their best, extremely beautiful and well-made pieces. The first of these factories were the Stevens Decoy Factory at Weedsport, Cayuga County, New York, and the Dodge Decoy Factory of Detroit, Michigan, started by Jasper N. Dodge in the 1880s. By far the most important and prolific factory, however, was Mason's Decoy Factory, also of Detroit, which existed from 1899 to 1926. The quality of their decoys, in the various grades starting with 'Premier' at the top, down through 'Challenge' and so on, were not equalled by any other factory.

Prints

From the point of view of the collector, 17th- and 18th-century American prints are only of historical and academic interest since it would be impossible today to build anything like a comprehensive collection. Most of the early examples have survived in very small numbers of impressions, some of them even being unique, and almost all of these have long since passed into museums from which they are not likely to emerge. It should also be remarked that until the 19th century, American printmakers rarely occupied themselves with producing historical or genre scenes, the majority of early prints being portraits.

The great family of New England divines, the Mathers, loomed large in the activities of early American printmakers. The first American print is John Foster of Dorchester, Massachusetts' woodcut portrait of Richard Mather (1596–1669), the first American copperplate engraving is Thomas Emmes of Boston's portrait of Increase Mather (1639–1727), whilst the first American mezzotint engraving is Peter Pelham's portrait of Cotton Mather (1663–1728). It is worth adding that eleven out of a total of fourteen known portraits by Pelham are of Boston clergymen.

By an ironic twist of fate, however, the most famous and sought-after American 18th-century print, Paul Revere Jnr's *The Bloody Massacre perpetrated in King Street Boston on March 5th, 1770*, is also one of the most common engravings of the period, and one a collector should have little difficulty in purchasing, assuming he has sufficient funds! As is well-known, Revere's print was cribbed directly, and somewhat dishonestly, from the almost identical composition by Henry Pelham called *The Fruits of Arbitrary Power, or The Bloody Massacre*, whilst Revere's print was copied in turn by Jonathan Mulliken, and other anonymous American and

96 Winslow Homer, *Eight Bells*, etching,
first edition, 1887. Generally considered one of
the very greatest 19th-century American prints.

English printmakers. Looking at Revere's somewhat crude and childlike drawing style, it is amazing to think that he was also the most sophisticated silversmith of his age.

American printmaking in the 19th century is dominated by the firm of Nathaniel Currier and James Merritt Ives. The first experiments with the art of lithography in America were carried out by Bass Otis between 1817 and 1819, and in 1824 William and John Pendleton started a commercial press in Boston. This firm took on the fifteen-year-old Nathaniel Currier in 1828. Six years later, he and his partner Stodart opened their own business in New York on Wall Street.

This only lasted a few months and in 1835, Currier set up on his own on Nassau Street. Popular success came in 1840 when his lurid depiction of the sinking of the steamship *Lexington* achieved an immense sale. Ives did not join the firm until 1852, being taken on as a bookkeeper. The celebrated partnership of Currier and Ives lasted from 1865 until 1907.

The popularity of Currier and Ives' prints lies in the fact that they were produced in large numbers, were inexpensive, and colourfully depicted scenes of American life in a unique and vivid way. The partnership attempted to carry out the popular motto of 'Art for the people', and chose a wide range of subject-matter to appeal to all tastes. They selected several important artists to design their prints, perhaps the most famous of whom was Arthur F. Tait, the animal painter, **97** whose depictions of the 'Noble Stag' betray his indebtedness to Landseer. Hunting scenes, coaching scenes and views of steamships on the Mississippi–these are the images which immediately spring to mind. It should be noted that the colouring of the lithographs was applied by hand.

Between 1827 and 1838, four double-elephant folio volumes of aquatints depicting birds were published in Scotland by a middle-aged French-American from New Orleans who had **86** been born on the island of Haiti. The achievement of John James Laforest Audubon in producing the 435 plates of *The Birds of America*, each one of which was hand-coloured by one or more of fifty colourists employed especially for the task, is one of the most remarkable feats of single-minded dedication in the history of art. The volumes cost the enormous sum of $100,000 to produce, and sold on subscription for $1,000 a set. Although this magnificent work ensured Audubon's fame, it did not make him a fortune. Today, it is one of the most admired of all colour-plate books; in 1969, Sotheby's in London sold a superb copy in almost mint condition for £90,000 ($216,000).

The unbelievable difficulties Audubon suffered in publishing *The Birds of America* and his success in achieving his aim, have contributed to the legendary aura which surrounds it. Approximately 175 sets were printed, although complete copies are now rare. The quality of the printing itself, whilst of a high standard, cannot be compared with that achieved in France by Redouté and others, and modern science has shown that, even though Audubon drew all the birds from actual specimens, his knowledge of ornithological

97 Currier & Ives print, *The Great Mississippi Steamboat Race*. The race was run from New Orleans to St Louis in July 1870, and was won by the Robert E. Lee. The American Museum in Britain, Bath.

science was very limited and many of the plates are inaccurate. For all this, the best of Audubon's work has a beauty and dramatic power unequalled in the history of colour-plate books. His knowledge of ornithology may have been slight but his aesthetic sensibility was faultless. Individual prints from this breathtaking book are now amongst the most highly regarded of all American graphics and rightly so.

In the second half of the 19th century, many of the leading European and American painters began making prints. Although there is a long tradition of the painter-printer, going back to Dürer and Rembrandt in the 16th and 17th centuries, and continuing with such artists as Tiepolo, Canaletto and Goya in the 18th century, many of the greatest painters did not in fact make prints themselves but allowed professional engravers to produce prints after their paintings. In the late 19th century, however, many painters took a deep interest in printing techniques, especially the French Impressionists and Post-Impressionists.

Two great American ex-patriates, Whistler and Mary Cassatt, are celebrated for their etchings and lithographs, while in America, Winslow Homer produced a small group 96 of etched works, which are justly considered amongst the masterpieces of American printmaking. Such prints appealed to an educated cultural elite and did not, of course, aim for popular success in the same way as Currier and Ives' lithographs.

An interesting use to which block-printing was put, a use which may be described fairly as a kind of 'folk printing' was in the decoration of hat boxes and the like. Such colourful 95 pieces were produced mainly in the first half of the 19th century, reaching their apogee in the 1830s. The boxes, usually oviform, were made of thin wood covered in brightly printed paper, showing scenes of everday life, history, famous buildings and landmarks. These crude yet colourful pieces are printed in a predominantly bluish colour, and as well as the kind of subjects listed above, were also produced for anniversaries and to commemorate special events. Thus Jenny Lind's American tour in the early 1850s was remembered by a block-printed hat box. Owing to the fact that boxes of this kind were in regular use, most of the surviving examples are in a rather poor condition.

AMERICAN ART AND THE COLLECTOR

Throughout this book, we have noted that American applied art depends stylistically upon European aesthetics. In no way should this be taken as a denegration of American craftsmanship. The richness of European culture was, and still is, devolved from a close interaction of craftsmen from the various major cities. English silver in the 17th and 18th centuries, for instance, drew heavily upon Dutch and French styles, German gunmakers influenced the whole of Europe in the 17th century, whilst French 18th-century art was considered the very type and mirror throughout Europe, although most of the great furniture-makers active in Paris were either Germans or Flemings. Although English silversmiths and cabinetmakers raised their respective crafts to a high level, they were still very conscious of what was happening in France, which was certainly not the case in reverse.

American culture was a unique fusion of European aesthetics, deriving from the French Huguenots, the English Puritans, the Germans and the Dutch. It may be safely said that from the 17th century onwards, the four countries listed here produced most of the finest European applied art, and their presence in a New World which, whilst forging its own national identity, also enabled the immigrants to retain certain native characteristics, ensured that American decorative art could borrow all that was best in Europe and create something uniquely its own. The fact that, with very few exceptions, American applied art has stylistic features which immediately manifest its origin, is proof of this.

The late 19th century, however, saw a change in direction. American craftsmen of the top rank began to rely less upon European influences and began to produce works of art in a spirit of aesthetic independence. Indeed, from the days of Tiffany & Company, Louis Comfort Tiffany and Frank Lloyd Wright at the turn of the century, American applied art, and latterly fine art, has come to have a greater influence in Europe than *vice versa*. With the advent of the New York School of painting in the late 1940s, there can be little doubt that the artistic focus of the Western world has become firmly centred in North America. This artistic independence in so comparatively young a country is a phenomenon as remarkable as America's economic and political development.

As for the antiques of the future—who can say? It is doubtful whether anyone in the 1920s would have imagined that within fifty years, Kewpie Dolls would be worthy of a place in a serious collector's cabinet. In a recent study of the Pop painter Andy Warhol, one writer pointed out that the green Coca-Cola bottles, which are so much a part of Warhol's early iconography, have not been produced for many years and, as is often the case with ephemera, are fairly scarce today, even though at one time they were produced in their millions. It is perfectly possible that an early Coca-Cola bottle will be just as significant an object for a collector in the future as a Kewpie Doll, or a 19th-century glass pictorial flask, also produced in absolutely vast quantities, are today.

On a more serious level, recent exhibitions of modern American ceramics have shown that this is an area still attracting some very fine craftsmen, whilst on the West Coast, many artist-craftsmen are producing superb ceramics, glass and furniture. The situation in America as regards the applied arts is certainly more healthy at the moment than it is in Europe and, mass-production methods notwithstanding, it seems certain that the collector of the future will have at least as rich and varied a selection of fine works of art to choose from as the collector of today.

ACKNOWLEDGEMENTS

My thanks are due to a number of dealers and collectors who have given help and provided photographs: James Dugdale, whose knowledge of birds is encyclopaedic; John Jesse in London; Elizabeth Mankin of Side Door Antiques, Kent, Connecticut; James Craig of Craig & Tarlton, Raleigh, North Carolina; Louis Lyons of New York; Phyllis Lucas of the Old Print Center, New York; Bard H. Langstaff of S. J. Shrubsole Corporation, New York and M. Freeman of I. Freeman & Son, Inc., of New York.

Several of the cool young ladies at Sotheby Parke-Bernet, New York, have been of the greatest help in locating and providing photographs, most notably the ever-patient Tish Roberts, who has been unfailingly kind and efficient; Adella Lowry, who gave me much valued advice; Ruth Ziegler and Joan Phillips. Norman Jones, head of the photographic department of Sotheby & Co. in London, provided some magnificent transparencies, as did Philippe Garner of Sotheby's-Belgravia. Miss Eleanor Hughes and John Culme, both of Sotheby's silver department, were also most helpful.

Mrs Coral Hull of the Corning Museum of Glass, Corning, New York and Mrs Gonin of the American Museum in Britain provided information on objects in their museums, as did the staff of the Art Institute of Chicago, and the Henry Francis du Pont Winterthur Museum.

Ian Bennett

The following books have been quoted in the text:

Joseph Downs, *American Furniture, the Queen Anne and Chippendale Periods*, The Macmillan Company, New York, 1952.

Harold F. Guilland, *American Folk Pottery*, Chilton Book Company, Philadelphia, New York, London, 1971.

Graham Hood, *American Silver*, Praeger Publishers, New York, 1971.

George S. and Helen McKearin, *American Glass*, Crown Publishers Inc., New York, 1971.

Charles F. Montgomery, *American Furniture, the Federal Period*, Thames and Hudson, London, 1967.

John G. Shea, *The American Shakers and their Furniture*, Van Nostrand Reinhold Company, New York, 1971.

Sources of photographs:

Ian Bennett, London 48, 80, 83, 84; Christie, Manson & Wood, London 41, 42, 43; Cooper-Bridgeman Library 24, 25, 26, 40, 73, 79; Corning Museum of Glass, Corning, New York 61, 62, 63, 64, 66; Craig & Tarlton, Raleigh, North California 19, 20; The Henry Francis du Pont Winterthur Museum, Winterthur, Delaware 18, 93; The Essex Institute, Salem, Massachusetts 87; Henry Ford Museum and Greenfield Village, Dearborn, Michigan 85; I. Freeman & Son, Inc., New York 52, 53, 54; Hamlyn Group Picture Library 23, 30, 88, 97; Louis Lyons, New York 57, 58, 59, 68, 71; Metropolitan Museum of Art, New York 1, 4; W. Keith Neal, London 82; New York Historical Society, New York 39; New York Public Library, Prints Division, Astor, Lenox and Tilden Foundations 2; Shelburne Museum, Shelburne, Vermont 95; S. J. Shrubsole Corp., New York 32, 34, 37, 44, 49; Sotheby & Co., London 27, 38, 46, 47, 60, 72, 86; Sotheby Parke-Bernet, New York endpapers, 3, 5, 7, 8, 9, 10, 11, 12, 13, 14, 15, 16, 17, 21, 22, 28, 29, 31, 33, 35, 36, 45, 50, 51, 56, 67, 69, 70, 74, 75, 76, 77, 78, 81, 89, 90, 91, 92, 94, 96; Sotheby's-Belgravia, London 55, 65.

INDEX

The numbers in italics refer to illustrations

CRANDALL'S LIVELY HORSEMAN.